ATLA BIBLIOGRAPHY SERIES
edited by Dr. Kenneth E. Rowe

UNCONSCIOUS:

A GUIDE TO THE SOURCES

by
Natalino Caputi

ATLA Bibliography Series, No. 16

**The American Theological
Library Association
and
The Scarecrow Press, Inc.
Metuchen, N.J., & London
1985**

Library of Congress Cataloging in Publication Data

Caputi, Natalino.
    Unconscious, a guide to the sources.

    (ATLA bibliography series ; no. 16)
    Includes index.
    1. Subconsciousness--Bibliography. I. Caputi,
Natalino. Guide to the unconscious. II. Title.
III. Series.
Z7204.S83C36 1985   [BF315]   016.154   85-1979
ISBN 0-8108-1798-5

★ CONTENTS ★

★ EDITOR'S NOTE ★

The American Theological Library Association Bibliography
series is designed to stimulate and encourage the preparation
of reliable bibliographies and guides to the literature of religious studies in all of its scope and variety. Compilers
are free to define their field, make their own selections,
and work out internal organization as the unique demands of
the subject require. We are pleased to publish Natalino
Caputi's bibliography as number 16 in the series.

Mr. Caputi took his undergraduate studies at Boston College
and Fairleigh Dickinson University, where he majored in
Psychology. Following studies in religious education at the
Unification Theological Seminary, he completed doctoral work
at Drew University. Mr. Caputi has joined Bernard Holdane
Associates, a career consulting firm in Morristown, New
Jersey, where he serves as a career consultant.

Kenneth E. Rowe
Series Editor

Drew University Library
Madison, New Jersey

★ PREFACE ★

The construct of the unconscious has raised more questions
than it was supposed to have answered. The numerous attempts to clarify the term have really only added to the confusion regarding the topic. This has been the case because
the word "unconscious" means different things to different
people and there hasn't been much consensus. The idea of
the unconscious is a controversial one on campus and a fas-
cinating one off-campus. It seems that virtually everyone
has some notion or at least an interest regarding the unconscious.

Granting the confusion and interest that surrounds the
topic of the unconscious, the questions still remain and continue to be raised; namely, what is the unconscious, is it,
where is it, why is it, and how is it? In an effort to address these questions I wrote the book Guide to the Unconscious.* The present work, Unconscious: A Guide to the
Sources, is a bibliographic sequel to the Guide. The former
book is a virtual catalogue organized according to a four-
factor typology of theorists and ideas regarding the unconscious. It is a first in terms of kind and scope. The Guide,
however, features no bibliography, and without one is incom-
plete as a reference tool. The serious researcher is still
left scrambling for more sources. This bibliography is the
complete document of references on the topic of the unconscious.

The bibliography is an invaluable tool for purposes of
research, teaching, and discussion. When one considers
how interdisciplinary the construct of the unconscious is one
can then appreciate the value of this comprehensive reference
book. Such a book has been long overdue. Just how interdisciplinary is the construct? A brief inspection of the entries reveals that the unconscious is relevant to the following

---

*Natalino Caputi, Guide to the Unconscious. Birmingham,
Alabama: Religious Education Press, 1984.

areas: Psychology, Philosophy, Religious Studies, Art, Literary Studies, Anthropology, Sociology, Education, Political Studies, Ethics, and Creativity. Also notice the diversity of journals that have featured articles on the unconscious. What is even more interesting to observe is just how many different topics have been analyzed in terms of some notion of the unconscious. I invite the reader to search the index for such subjects.

The value of the bibliography is also demonstrated by simply comparing the card catalogue on the topic of any two or more libraries. There is very little consistency between one library and other regarding what items are included as entries for the topic of the unconscious. The bibliography will solve this problem because now the topic of the unconscious has its first, central reference text.

Natalino Caputi
Boonton, N. J.
March 24, 1984

★ INTRODUCTION ★

"Suddenly, psychology is excited again about
the unconscious. " (Daniel Goleman, New York
Times, February 7, 1984, p. C1)

One dramatic way to appreciate the present condition regarding the topic of the unconscious is to look up the word in the
index.   There one is confronted by a multitude of adjectival
and noun form usages of the expression "unconscious. "   The
immediate question becomes "How can there be so many unconsciouses?"   One would believe that there would or could
only be one unconscious.   The question becomes even more
ironic when one discovers that the existence of any unconscious is still an unsettled issue.

The state of the topic of the unconscious, in the literature, is marked by multiplicity, ambiguity, confusion, and
selectivity.   The first three attributes are apparent after one
does the exercise suggested in the first paragraph.   Selectivity refers to the fact that writers on the subject tend to favor
certain understandings of what the unconscious is and exclude
or fail to mention the other ways the construct is understood
and related to their particular understanding of it.   Also there
is a tendency to believe that Sigmund Freud and Carl Jung
have said all there is about the unconscious.   True, they
made significant contributions; true, the literature on the unconscious is filled with their names and ideas; but it is also
true that many other theorists have said other things about
the unconscious.   This bibliography is proof of that.

The confusion surrounding the topic of the unconscious
is matched only by the expressed sense of importance that
writers give to the construct.   They write about the unconscious that it is the most vital aspect of an individual, of
groups of people, and even of all life.   To ignore the unconscious is to suffer without knowing why.   To know about it
can mean power, solutions to problems, freedom, self-
knowledge, dreams coming true, contact with God, and so

forth. The list of potentials and powers of the unconscious goes on and on. Again, the question comes up, How can something seemingly so important be in such a state of confusion? Our degree of certain knowledge about the unconscious has yet to do justice to the felt importance of what the unconscious is and means to life and human behavior.

In an effort to answer some of the questions about the unconscious an investigation was initiated whereby a large net was cast to collect the many different ideas on the subject. This bibliography is the end result of the extensive search through the literature on the unconscious. On the foundation of the bibliography the book Guide to the Unconscious was written. In that book the wide and wild world of ideas about the unconscious was submitted to a topological approach. The Guide features a comprehensive typology which subsumes virtually all points of view and represents an update on the state of the topic of the unconscious.

The method being typology, the intent was to identify and distinguish characteristic types of approaches toward the understanding of the unconscious. What was discovered after reviewing the vast literature was that essentially only one or more of four fundamental types of approaches could be discerned. Each approach features a unique understanding of the unconscious.

There are four basic ways of speaking about the unconscious which, by appreciating these four ways, serve well to order the great disparity and variety of opinions, conceptions, and theories about the unconscious. In sum, we have four approaches and four types of unconsciouses. The four approaches have been designated the Bio-Physical Approach, Psycho-Personal Approach, Socio-Cultural Approach, and Transpersonal-Spiritual Approach. A brief description of each will follow.

The Bio-Physical Approach deals with an unconscious that is related to and written about in terms of the subtle processes that are a direct function of our physical body. These are the unconscious processes having to do with our biology, nervous system, and instincts. Under this category, theorists who explicitly write in terms of a theory of the unconscious have been involved in researching such things as memory functions, automatic behavior, conditioning, subliminal events, and the physical foundation (even "site") of the unconscious. The implication is that the unconscious is a function of these processes or that the unconscious is the agent responsible for some phenomena related to these functions. In this type of literature one will read about such expressions as Physiological Unconscious, Vital Unconscious, Instinctual Unconscious, Perceptive Unconscious, Lower Unconscious, Organic Unconscious, and so forth. Despite the neologisms one will find, upon closer inspection it can be seen that the theorist is investigating behavior or events in terms of our previous list of areas such as memory, automatism, and so forth.

The Psycho-Personal Approach features an unconscious that is essentially derived from and a function of an individual's emotional and cognitive development. Here the emphasis is on the more psychological factors related to one's personal history. The primary focus here is on such things as memories, feelings, thought processes, and ideations. The biophysical dimension is not denied, but it is not the focus of attention in this approach. If we can say that the Bio-Physical type of unconscious is more typical of the experimental laboratory, the Psycho-Personal type is a product of the psychotherapeutic couch and clinic. In the literature which makes up the Psycho-Personal Approach one will come across such expressions as Deep Psychological Unconscious, Emotional Unconscious, Cognitive Unconscious, Personal Unconscious, Freudian Unconscious, Acquired Unconscious, Psychodynamic Unconscious, Preconscious, Rational Unconscious, and so forth. Regardless of the neologism, the center of attention in the Psycho-Personal Approach is latent, hidden, or subtle emotional-cognitive processes.

The Socio-Cultural Approach involves an unconscious that is understood to be a function of a collectivity, such as a crowd, a group, an association, a race, or a nation. Those who write within this framework speak of the unconscious as something that emerges or comes into being when individuals group themselves for various but definite and common reasons. The gathering and associating of people is the necessary condition for this type of unconscious to manifest itself. Within the Socio-Cultural Approach the unconscious can also stand for that part of the individual psyche that is common to all individuals. In a sense it refers to the record of the psychic evolution and history of a particular group or race. In this type of literature one will encounter such expressions as Collective Unconscious, Collective Preconscious, Common Unconscious, Racial Unconscious, Collective Psyche, Master Mind, National Soul, and so forth. With the Socio-Cultural Approach we move from the realm of the individual to the social dimension and expression of the unconscious.

The Transpersonal-Spiritual Approach deals with an unconscious that is understood to be a transpersonal entity or a medium or means to contact transpersonal entities and dimensions. When the unconscious is written about as an "outside" entity it is seen in bigger-than-life terms. In fact, in these instances the word "unconscious" is usually capitalized and sometimes it reads "The Unconscious." As such The Unconscious is an entity that not only is the source of all life but even orchestrates all life activities human and nonhuman according to some destiny or plan. In more modest terms the unconscious is seen as some agent or power within an individual that possesses special abilities to obtain many things, . such as solutions to problems, inspiration, wealth, health, healing, and so on. The unconscious is seen as a fantastic converting agent that can make dreams and desires become a reality. Virtually every bookstore, in the "self-help" section, will feature at least a dozen books on how to achieve x, y, and z by learning how to use one's unconscious mind. On the more spiritual side the Transpersonal-Spiritual type of unconscious is understood as our contact point with God and the spiritual world. When God speaks to us, it is through the unconscious. When we pray it is through the unconscious that prayers are sent and answers received. In sum, the Transpersonal-Spiritual type of unconscious is the explanation for parapsychological, paranormal, and supernatural events. Some neologisms associated with this type include Synchronistic Unconscious, Absolute Unconscious, Collective Unconscious, Higher Unconscious, Trans-Individual Unconscious, Teleological Unconscious, Super-Conscious, Objective Psyche, Cosmic Unconscious, and so forth. The bigger-than-life dimension of this type is obvious.

With the preceding typology in hand one can now better identify, understand, and relate the various theorists and ideas regarding the unconscious. A book or article entitled "The Unconscious" tells us very little. Our immediate question is, What approach and type is the author working with? Some theorists deal exclusively with one approach and type. Others involve two or more approaches. Still others include all four types. We now have a way to sort out the various ideas. Properly distinguished, theories concerning the unconscious coming out of one approach can be better appreciated by theorists working in another approach. The confusion that is usually associated with the topic of the unconscious need no longer exist because now we have a tool to understand what is being said about the unconscious.

A word needs to be said about the terms "subconscious" and "unconscious." Are the two expressions referring to two things or one? Some writers use one expression rather than the other. Because of this practice the index to this bibliography distinguishes the two terms for those interested in who uses what expression. Some theorists will explain why they prefer one term over the other. Others who use both expressions in one system of ideas will distinguish them. Many times the two expressions are used carelessly, that is, without distinction. They are used as if they mean the same thing, but it is never made clear so sometimes one gets the impression that the unconscious and the subconscious are two different things. Notwithstanding everything just mentioned, in doing the research for this book, the expressions "unconscious" and "subconscious" were treated as synonymous terms. They can be regarded as two words with the same meaning unless otherwise specified vis-à-vis a particular theorist.

To conclude this introduction, if the opening quotation is a correct reading of the situation—that is, that psychology is indeed excited again about the unconscious—it is vital to the ongoing discussion and investigation of the unconscious to have a basic text. This book is the sourcebook. With it the renewed excitement over the unconscious can result in a better understanding of what the construct refers to and how it is significant for the psychology of human behavior. The fog of confusion that presently surrounds the topic can be lifted.

★ A GUIDE TO SOURCES ★

Most of the entries in this bibliography have
been identified according to the typology outlined in the Introduction.

1. Abadi, E. "Le docteur invraisemblable, notre incon-
    scient, les choses et nous. " (The improbable doc-
    tor, our unconsciousness, objects, and ourselves.)
    La psychologie et la vie 6 (1932): 12-13.

2. Abend, S. M. "Unconscious fantasy and theories of
    cure. " Journal of American Psychoanalytic Asso-
    ciation 27, no. 3 (1979): 579-96. Two cases are
    presented to discuss how a patient's, as well as the
    therapist's, theory of cure influences the progress
    of the therapy, and how both are based on uncon-
    scious sexual fantasies. (Psycho-Personal Approach)

3. Aberdam, R. "Le subconscient selon la psychologie in-
    dividuelle. " (The subconsciousness according to in-
    dividual psychology.) La psychologie et la vie 6
    (1932): 25-27. The theories of Adler and Freud
    are contrasted. (Psycho-Personal Approach)

4. Abrams, S. "The Psychoanalytic Unconscious. " In The
    Unconscious Today, pp. 207-210. Edited by M.
    Kranzer. New York: International Universities
    Press, 1971. (Psycho-Personal Approach)

5. Ach, N. "Ueber den Begriff des Unbewussten in der
    Psychologie der Gegenwart. " (The concept of the
    unconscious in contemporary psychology.) Zeitschrift
    für Psychologie 129 (1933): 223-45.

6. Ack, Marvin. "Toward understanding irrationality. "
    Menninger Quarterly 23, no. 2 (Summer 1969): 2-13.
    It is argued that a theory of the unconscious can
    help in understanding irrational behavior.

7. Adams, Virginia. "'Mommy and I are One'; Beaming messages to inner space." Psychology Today (May 1982): 24-36. By "inner space" Adams is referring to the unconscious. This article is a commentary on the work of Lloyd Silverman, who used a tachistoscope to flash messages subliminally and observed the effect on the person. (Bio-Physical Approach). See also Lloyd Silverman.

8. Adler, Alfred. The Individual Psychology of Alfred Adler. Edited by Heinz Ansbacker. New York: Basic Books, 1956. The book features no section on Adler's views about the unconscious. Adler avoided the use of the expression. He preferred to consider that there were aspects of a person's lifestyle that were not yet understood by the person. The few places that Adler does comment explicitly regarding the unconscious can be found by referring to the editor's index. In fact, the editor has written an article precisely on the topic of Adler and the unconscious (see Heinz Ansbacker). (Psycho-Personal Approach)

9. Adler, G. "Study of a dream. A contribution to the concept of the collective unconscious and to the technique of analytical psychology." British Journal of Medical Psychology 19 (1941): 56-72. (Psycho-Personal Approach)

10. Airapetyantz, E., and K. Bykov. "Physiological experiments and the psychology of the subconscious." Philosophy and Phenomenological Research 5 (1945): 577-93. In the article many Russian experiments are cited. This work is based on I. Pavlov's and I. Sechenov's ideas on conditioned reflexes and interoceptive conditioning. The point regarding the subconscious is that conditioning can take place with the internal environment of the organism and that such conditioning can influence behavior subliminally. These subliminally conditioned reflexes are bases of what the subconscious refers to. (Bio-Physical Approach)

11. Allendy, R. "La part de la psychanalyse dans la connaissance de l'inconscient." (The part played by psychoanalysis in a knowledge of the unconscious.) La psychologie et la vie 6 (1932): 18-20. (Psycho-Personal Approach)

12. Altschule, M. "The growth of the concept of unconscious cerebration before 1890." In Roots of Modern
Psychiatry, pp. 56-83. New York: Grune & Stratton, 1965. This is a short historical study on the
topic with many theorists mentioned. (Bio-Physical
and Psycho-Personal Approaches)

13. Altvater, Nancy B. "An experimental study of a conscious or an unconscious stimulus and its influence
on children's art expression." Ed. D dissertation,
University of Kansas, 1965.

14. Ammon, Günter, and Wolfgang Rock. "The unconscious
structuring and the group-dependent development of
personality." Dynamische Psychiatrie 12, no. 5
(1979): 377-94. The article discusses the integration of the theoretical, sociological, and biological
aspects of personality as understood by the Berlin
School.

15. Amosov, N. M. Modelirovanie myshleniya i psikhiki.
(Simulation of thinking and of the psyche.) Kiev,
USSR: Naukova Dumka, 1965. The author conducts
a cybernetic exposition involving the simulation of
the subconscious with the use of computers. (Bio-
Physical Approach)

16. Anbender, Kenneth. "Conceptions of unconscious process." Ph. D. dissertation, Adelphi University, 1975.
Anbender argues that historically the theories of unconscious processes seemed to have followed a similar pattern of development as that described by Carl
Jung in regard to how the ego comes to terms with
the unconscious. In other words, at first the unconscious is perceived to be threatening, then to have
progressive elements, and finally to be the very
source of the ego. Various theories are presented
according to this model.

17. Anderson, J. "The genesis of social reactions in the
young child." In The Unconscious, A Symposium,
pp. 69-90. Edited by C. M. Child. New York:
Alfred A. Knopf, 1927. Anderson describes how
habits operate with more and more automaticity. He
prefers to speak about patterns of learned responses
rather than some reified notion of the unconscious.
(Psycho-Personal Approach)

18. (Anon.) "D'après J. Froebes les modalités du subcon-
    scient." (The modalities of the subconscious accord-
    ing to J. Froebes.) La psychologie et la vie 6 (1932):
    4-5. This deals with subconscious sensations and
    pathological dissociation. (Psycho-Personal Approach)

19. Ansbacker, Heinz L. "Adler's views on the uncon-
    scious." Journal of Individual Psychology 38, no. 1
    (March 1982): 32-41. (Psycho-Personal Approach).
    See item no. 8

20. Anscombe, R. "Referring to the unconscious: A philo-
    sophical critique of Schafer's action language."
    International Journal of Psychoanalysis 62, part 2
    (1981): 225-41. Anscombe presents and criticizes
    Schafer's theory that the "person" is the sole agent of
    action and not one who is acted upon by fragmentary
    unconscious psychic aspects. (Psycho-Personal
    Approach)

21. Ansell, C. "The unconscious: Agency of the occult."
    Psychoanalytic Review 53, no. 4 (1966): 164-72.
    Ansell looks at cases of telepathy and clairvoyance
    from a Freudian perspective. He asks whether the
    metapsychology of psychoanalysis can accommodate
    the experiences in question. The best he does is to
    suggest the possible motivational foundation of tele-
    pathic and clairvoyant experiences. (Psycho-Personal
    Approach)

22. Arden, Eugene. "Hawthorne's 'Case of Arthur D.'"
    American Imago 18 (1961): 45-55. The Scarlet
    Letter is investigated for its implicit psychology of
    of the unconscious. (Psycho-Personal Approach)

23. Arieti, Silvano. "Cognitive components in human con-
    flict and unconscious motivation." Journal of the
    American Academy of Psychoanalysis 5, no. 1
    (1977): 5-16. Arieti is arguing against the exclusive
    reduction of psychogenic motivation to instincts and
    for the role of ideas, self-image, and meaning of
    one's life as motivational factors. He accuses both
    psychoanalysis and behavior therapy for under-
    estimating the importance of cognitive components
    in human behavior. (Psycho-Personal Approach)

24. Arnold, St. George Tucker. "Consciousness and the
    unconscious in the fiction of Eudora Welty." Ph.D.

dissertation, Stanford University, 1975. Arnold draws upon the scholarship of Carl Jung, Erich Neumann, and ideas in mythology to present an analysis of Eudora Welty's early fiction. The general theme expressed is the ongoing struggle of the psyche toward wholeness and integration.

25. Asmolov, A. G. "Classification of unconscious phenomena and the category of activity." Soviet Psychology 19, no. 3 (Spring 1981): 29-45. The three types are 1) supraindividual, supraconscious phenomena; 2) unconscious motives and the associated semantic personality sets; and 3) unconscious mechanisms of regulation.

26. Assagioli, Roberto. Psychosynthesis. New York: Viking Press, 1965. In the early pages of this book Assagioli maps out his picture of the human psyche which includes the Lower Unconscious, Middle Unconscious, Higher Unconscious, Conscious, the I, the Higher Self, and the Collective Unconscious. (Assagioli deals with all four types of unconsciouses.)

27. _____. "Jung and psychosynthesis." Journal of Humanistic Psychology 14, no. 1 (Win 1974): 35-55. Assagioli compares and contrasts Jung's ideas with his own.

28. Aveling, F. "Is the conception of the unconscious of value in psychology?" Mind 31 (1922): 423-33. Aveling considers the construct of the unconscious to be useful because something must be supposed in the place of processes which do not occur in awareness to explain what sometimes does happen in awareness. This article is one of a three-part discussion. See also G. C. Field and J. Laird. (Psycho-Personal Approach)

29. Bailey, Keels D. "The contribution of the psychoanalytic theory of symbolic thinking to understanding the unconscious roots of prejudice." Th. D. dissertation, School of Theology at Claremont, 1967. Some of the unconscious mechanisms of prejudice discussed are 1) symbolic thinking whereby one splits good and bad, condenses goodness and badness into such symbols as white and black, projects the badness outside oneself, and displaces the badness from one object to another; 2) the need to protect oneself from forbidden (oral,

anal, and phallic) impulses by projecting them onto the Negro. (Psycho-Personal Approach)

30. Baker, James V. "The subterranean fountain: The role of the unconscious in Coleridge's theory of imagination." Ph. D. dissertation, University of Michigan, 1954.

31. Baker, Sidney J. "The mathematics of the unconscious." Journal of Clinical Experimental Psychopathology 12 (1951): 192-212. The author attempts to demonstrate that the unconscious or preconscious mind can perform mathematical operations distinct from the conventional kind. Baker is working within a psychoanalytic framework. (Psycho-Personal Approach)

32. Balzac, H. Unconscious Humorists. New York: Century, 1904.

33. Bär, Eugen S. "The language of the unconscious according to Jacques Lacan." Ph. D. dissertation, Yale University, 1971. According to Bär, Lacan reveals psychoanalysis to be predominantly a linguistic discipline. Bär contends, though, that Lacan's linguistic model of unconscious processes needs considerable clarification to do justice to the experiences in question. (Psycho-Personal Approach)

34. Barchilon, Jose. "On countertransference 'cures'." Journal of American Psychoanalytic Association 6 (1958): 222-36. Jose discusses six cases wherein the unconscious of the therapist, not the patient's, facilitated the cure. (Psycho-Personal Approach)

35. Bargar, R., and J. Duncan. "Cultivating creative endeavor in doctoral research." Journal of Higher Education 53, no. 1 (Jan/Feb 1982): 1-31. This article contains a section entitled "The ego and the creative unconscious." The creative unconscious is discussed in terms of being the source of new ideas for research. (Psycho-Personal and Transpersonal-Spiritual Approaches)

36. Barker, R. C. The Power of Decision. New York: Dodd, Mead & Company, 1968. Barker makes use of a notion of the subconscious as an agent in helping to convert ideas into reality. (Transpersonal-Spiritual Approach)

37. Bartlett, Francis H. "Marxism and the psychoanalytic
theory of the unconscious." Science and Society 16
(1952): 44-52. Bartlett conducts a Marxist critique
and counterproposal to the Freudian construct of the
unconscious. The main point argued is that the
source of a person's problem does not lie in some
obscure "unconscious" but in the person's actual,
social practice, which one may not fully recognize or
may falsely perceive. This article should be read
along with Albert Starr's article because Bartlett,
in part, responded to Starr's ideas. (Psycho-Personal
Approach). See also Albert Starr.

38. Bash, K. W. "'Bewusstseins' schwund." (Loss of 'consciousness.') Nervenarzt 53, no. 11 (Nov 1982):
628-34. Both the bio-physical and the psycho-
personal understanding of the unconscious are discussed.

39. Bassin, F. V. "Mezhinstitutskoe soveshchanie pri
Prezidiume AMNSSR po voprosam ideologicheskoi
bor'by s sovremennym freidiamom." (Joint Institute
Conference organized by the Presidium of the USSR
Academy of Medical Sciences on Problems of the
Ideological Struggle with Contemporary Freudianism.)
Zhurnal Nevropatologii i Psikhiatrii 59 (1959): 636-
39. A conference was held in October 1958 to dis-
cuss ways of combating Freudianism. The contention
is that the construct of the unconscious and other
Freudian concepts should be given a materialist-
physiological interpretation along Pavlovian lines.
(Bio-Physical Approach)

40. _____. Problema bessoznatel'nogo. (The Problem of
the Unconscious.) Moscow: Izdatelstvo Meditsina,
1968. In this book Bassin refers to what he called
"uncognized forms of higher nervous activity" and
their role in biological regulation. He also discusses
the formation of sets, the processing of information,
and so forth. Bassin also discusses the problem of
the unconscious in general, the theories preceding
Freud, and a criticism of the psychoanalytic conceptions. (Bio-Physical Approach)

41. Bassin, F. V., and A. Sherozia. "The role of the
category of the unconscious in the system of the
present-day scientific knowledge of the mind." Paper
presented at the International Symposium on the

Problem of the Unconscious. Tbilisi, USSR in 1979.
The importance of the unconscious is admitted but
the tendency is to interpret the construct in terms
of bio-physical categories. There is evidence that
the beginning of a serious psycho-personal approach
was discussed. See item no. 690.

42. Baudouin, Charles. "L'inconscient dans la contemplation
esthetic." (The unconscious in esthetic contemplation.) Archives de psychologie 21 (1928): 55-75.
Using a case study of a painter Baudouin makes the
point that a work of art can serve the same purpose
as a dream. Baudouin prefers the expression "subconscious." (Transpersonal-Spiritual Approach)

43. _____. "La discipline du subconscient." (Discipline
of the subconscious.) Psychologie et la vie 6 (1932):
20-22. Suggestion and psychoanalysis are discussed
as methods that tend to discipline the subconscious.

44. _____. Suggestion and Autosuggestion. London:
George Allen & Union Ltd., 1954. The author uses
the construct of the subconscious to explain the
mechanics of suggestion and autosuggestion. Indeed,
it is the subconscious that is operative in phenomena
related to suggestion. (Transpersonal-Spiritual Approach)

45. Baynes, H. G. Germany Possessed. London: Jonathan
Cape, Ltd., 1941. Baynes employs a psychology of
the collective unconscious to speculate on the events
that occurred in Germany prior to and during World
War II. (Socio-Cultural Approach)

46. Beck, L., "Conscious and unconscious motives." Mind
75, no. 298 (Apr 1966): 155-79. Beck conducts a
very intricate discussion of motivation making many
distinctions regarding the possible answers to the
question of why a person does something. He argues
that the expression "unconscious motive" may seem
to be an oxymoron (a contradiction in terms), but
nevertheless it is a good expression for understanding
some behaviors. (Psycho-Personal Approach)

47. Beecher, Willard. "The myth of 'the unconscious'."
Individual Psychology Bulletin 8 (1950): 99-110. Two
myths are presented and criticized: that the uncon-

scious remembers everything and that the unconscious possesses its own will that opposes good intentions. Beecher argues for Adler's ideas about the unconscious. Adler does not use the construct of the unconscious and prefers to argue in terms of a lack of understanding of one's self and situation. (Psycho-Personal Approach)

48. Béguin, A. L'âme romantique et le reve. Paris: Librairie J. Corti, 1946. Béguin discusses dream interpretation within the Romantic tradition. (Transpersonal-Spiritual Approach)

49. Bellak, Leopold, ed. "Conceptual and methodological problems in psychoanalysis." Annals of the New York Academy of Sciences 76 (1959): 971-1134. Bellak and others critically reconsider various aspects of psycho-analytical theory (unconscious, and so forth) with the intent to update them and render them more empirically testable. (Psycho-Personal Approach)

50. _____. "The unconscious." Annals of the New York Academy of Sciences 76 (1959): 1066-97. Bellak is dealing here with meanings of the construct of the unconscious that are relevant to psychoanalysis. He distinguishes two aspects of the unconscious; namely, the "physiological unconscious" and the "configurational unconscious." (Psycho-Personal Approach)

51. Beloff, Halla, and John Beloff. "Unconscious self-evaluation using a stereoscope." Journal of Abnormal Social Psychology 59 (Sept 1959): 275-78. (Psycho-Personal Approach)

52. Benassy, M. "Psychanalyse théorique." (Theoretical psychoanalysis.) Bulletin de Psychologie 20, no. 8-9 (1967): 563-67. The author distinguishes Freud's construct of the unconscious with that of psychologists and the psychophysiologists.

53. Benda, C. E. "Das Unbewusste und der Aufbau der geistigen Welt." (The unconscious and the structure of the psychical world.) Allgemeine Zeitschrift für Psychiatrie 4 (1931): 7-19. Writing within a psychoanalytic framework Benda discusses the topic of the unconscious in terms of "Geist" and "Seele."

54. Bennis, W. The Unconscious Conspiracy. New York: AMACOM, 1976. There is no theoretical or other discussion of the unconscious per se. Bennis is dealing with some of the moral issues relating to large corporations. One point made is that large corporations make it possible for individuals to work toward ultimately immoral ends without an immediate sense of personal responsibility or guilt.

55. Bennitt, C. The Real Use of the Unconscious. New York: Dial Press, 1937. (Transpersonal-Spiritual Approach)

56. Berdorff, W. "Ludwig Klages und das Problem des Unbewussten." (Ludwig Klages and the problem of the unconscious.) Die neue deutsche Schule 2 (1928): 839-46.

57. Bergler, Edmund. "Unconscious mechanisms in 'writer's block'." Psychoanalytic Review 42 (1955): 160-67. (Psycho-Personal Approach)

58. Bernardi, Ricardo. "Word-presentation and thing-presentation in the Freudian conception of the unconscious." (In Spanish). Revista Uruguaya de Psicoanalisis 57 (Jan 1978): 111-24. (Psycho-Personal Approach)

59. Berry, Dianne D. "Conscious and unconscious mental states." Ph.D. dissertation, University of Oklahoma, 1979. Berry argues that Freud's theory of conscious and unconscious mental states is basically correct. (Psycho-Personal Approach)

60. Bertalanffy, Ludwig. "Mind and body re-examined." Journal of Humanistic Psychology (Fall 1966): 113-37. Essentially the article is a response to a Dr. Lach, who criticized Bertalanffy's article on the mind-body problem. Lach considered the unconscious a "grab-bag" name for unexplored physiological mechanisms. Bertalanffy cautions that equating the unconscious with only physiological mechanisms leads to a crude materialism. (Bio-Physical and Psycho-Personal Approaches)

61. Bettelheim, Bruno. Freud and Man's Soul. New York: Alfred A. Knopf, 1983. An attempt is made to show some connection between Freud's theory of the unconscious and the notion of "soul." (Psycho-Personal Approach)

62. Bigelow, Samuel T. "Thomas Carlyle's notion of the
     unconscious and its influence on his early writings."
     Ph.D. dissertation, Claremont Graduate School, 1972.
     Bigelow examines the Germanic sources for Carlyle's
     ideas about the unconscious. According to Bigelow,
     Carlyle was the first to formulate a general doctrine
     of the unconscious in English. The unconscious for
     Carlyle was the source of truth and inspiration and
     was the contact with God. (Transpersonal-Spiritual
     Approach)

63. Binswanger, Ludwig. "The Unconscious." In Being-in-
     the-World, pp. 84-101. Translated by J. Needleman.
     New York: Harper & Row, 1963. Here we get an
     understanding of what the unconscious means to the
     school of Daseinsanalysis. The unconscious, accord-
     ing to this school, is not some "thing" working behind
     the scenes, but the expression for certain hidden, not
     yet fully understood, aspects of one's life. (Psycho-
     Personal Approach)

64. Blakeslee, T. R. The Right Brain (A new understanding
     of the unconscious mind and its creative powers).
     Garden City, N.Y.: Anchor Press/Doubleday, 1980.
     This book is based on brain research dealing with the
     abilities and capabilities of the right and left hemi-
     spheres. Essentially Blakeslee argues that the non-
     dominant, right hemisphere is the seat of the uncon-
     scious and the source of creativity. (Bio-Physical
     Approach)

65. Bloor, C. "Some notes on memory." Psyche 8 (1928):
     89-96. Bloor writes about memory in terms of the
     notion of "traces" which survive and operate subcon-
     sciously. According to Bloor every experience leaves
     a trace and modifies the previous disposition of the
     organism. (Bio-Physical Approach)

66. Bodkin, A. "The subconscious factors of mental process
     considered in relation to thought." Mind 16, part I
     and II (1907): 209-28, 362-82. (Psycho-Personal
     Approach)

67. Bodkin, M. "Literary criticism and the study of the
     unconscious." Monist 37 (1927): 445-68. Bodkin
     draws upon the ideas of Freud, Jung, John Thorburn
     (Art and the Unconscious), and Frederick Prescott

(The Poetic Mind) to discuss the nature of creative expression.

68. Boe, John. "Pastoral and the unconscious." Ph.D. dissertation, University of California, Berkeley, 1974.

69. Bondarenko, P. P., and M. Rabinovich. "Nauchnoe soveshchanie po voprosam ideologicheskoi bor'by sovremennym freidiznom." (Scientific conference on problems of the ideological struggle with contemporary Freudism.) Voprosy Filosofii 13, no. 2 (1959): 164-70. Attempts are made to expose the fallacies of Freud's ideas. It is contended that the issue of unconscious motivation was also dealt with by Ivan Pavlov.

70. Booth, Gotthard. "Unconscious motivation in the choice of the ministry as vocation." Pastoral Psychology 9, no. 89 (1958): 18-24. The author draws upon the ideas of Freud, Szondi, and Jung to distinguish three levels of the unconscious mind or three levels of possible sources of motivation involved in the choice for the ministry. The three levels include childhood experiences, inherited psychological dispositions, and archetypal influences. (Psycho-Personal and Transpersonal-Spiritual Approaches)

71. Born, Wolfgang B. "Unconscious processes in artistic creation." Journal of Clinical Psychopathology and Psychology 7 (1945): 253-72. Born makes the point that the unconscious is the source of inspiration for a work of art. (Psycho-Personal Approach)

72. Bose, B. "The postulate of the un-conscious and some basic concepts of psychoanalysis." Samiksa 32, no. 3 (1978): 69-79. Bose argues for a more parsimonious accounting of certain phenomena based on a theory of psycho-physical parallelism instead of Freud's theory of the unconscious. The mind-body problem is the issue here. (Bio-Physical and Psycho-Personal Approaches)

73. Boss, M. "Le problem du moi dans la motivation." (The problem of the self in motivation.) Evolution Psychiatriques 25 (1960): 481-89. The theories of Freud, Jung, and Szondi are referred to. Boss maintains that unconscious content and unconscious

processes cannot be ignored in any inquiry regarding motivation. (Psycho-Personal Approach)

74. _____. "Daseinsanalytic re-evaluation of the basic concepts of psychoanalytic theory." In Psychoanalysis and Daseinsanalysis, pp. 75-129. New York: Basic Books, 1963.

75. Brauneck, A. E. "Das Unbewusste und die Affekte." (The unconscious and the emotions.) Psyche 35, no. 11 (Nov 1981): 1034-54.

76. Brenman, Margaret. "Tension systems and unconscious processes." Ph.D. dissertation, University of Kansas, 1942.

77. Brennan, Robert E. General Psychology; A Study of Man Based on St. Thomas Aquinas. New York: Macmillan, 1952. Although Aquinas never used the word "unconscious" he did write about the vegetative life and the sensitive life in a way that we could interpret as alluding to the unconscious. In fact, Paul Nolan devoted his dissertation to such a topic. (See also Paul Nolan.) Both authors are good references for tracing the idea of the unconscious before the word was actually coined.

78. Breton, André. Les Manifestos du Surréalisme. (Manifesto of Surrealism.) Paris: Le Sagittaire, 1955. Breton calls upon artists to explore the "unknown mind," and to utilize (paint) subconscious visions, dreams, and hallucinations. (Transpersonal-Spiritual Approach)

79. Brill, A. "Unconscious insight: some of its manifestations." International Journal of Psychoanalysis 10 (1929): 145-61. Brills presents many cases of unconscious adjustments made by people in order to handle struggles so that they can go on living. A Freudian framework is assumed. (Psycho-Personal Approach)

80. _____. "Freud's metapsychology." Hebrew Medical Journal 13 (1940): 177-89. The author devotes a good portion of this piece to the discussion of Freud's notion of "archaic inheritances," and the role of phylogeny. (Psycho-Personal and Social-Cultural Approaches)

81. Brinkmann, Donald. Problems des Unbewussten. Zurich: Raschen, 1943.

82. Bristol, Charles. "What the subconscious is." In The Magic of Believing, pp. 40-47. New York: Pocket Books, 1948. The subconscious is, according to Bristol, a powerful agent in making desires come true. (Transpersonal-Spiritual Approach)

83. Broden, A. R., and W. A. Myer. "Hypochondriacal symptoms as derivatives of unconscious fantasies of being beaten or tortured." Journal of the American Psychoanalytic Association 29, no. 3 (1981): 535-57.

84. Brodeur, Claude. Du problème de l'inconscient à une philosophie de l'homme: I. Les théories freudiennes sur la structure de l'organisme psychique. (The problem of the unconscious to a philosophy of man: I. The Freudian theories on the structure of the psychic organism.) Montreal: Institut de Recherches Psychologiques, 1968.

85. _____. Du problème de l'inconscient à une philosophie de l'homme: II. La structure de la pensée humaine. (The problem of the unconscious to a philosophy of man: II. The structure of human thought.) Montreal: Institut de Recherches Psychologiques, 1969.

86. Brody, Benjamin. "The denial of the unconscious: A great leap backward." International Journal of Psychiatry 8 (Aug 1969): 590-595.

87. Brown, Barbara. New Mind, New Body. New York: Bantam Books, 1974. Chapter three is entitled, "Skin talk: Conversations with the subconscious," and chapter eleven is entitled, "Identifying one's own brain waves: A trial run to the subconscious." This is an excellent book as an introduction to bio-feedback, but probably one of the most chaotic pieces regarding the theory of the unconscious. Brown uses the expressions "subconscious," "unconscious," "non-conscious," and "subliminal" carelessly, that is, without distinguishing her terms.

88. Bruck, Mark A. "The concept of 'the unconscious'." Individual Psychology Bulletin 8 (1950): 81-98.

Freud's predecessors are presented regarding the
concept of the unconscious. Bruck also discusses the
theoretical differences between Freudian and Adlerian
approaches. (Psycho-Personal Approach)

89.   Brugmans, H. J. "The psychic unconscious and the
      psychological unconscious." Acta Psychologica 4
      (1939): 241-70.

90.   Brunton, P. The Quest of the Overself. New York:
      Dutton, 1938. Brunton adapts an oriental method of
      psychospiritual self-analysis to Western ways of
      thinking. The so-called "overself" has some relation-
      ship to what others refer to as the unconscious.

91.   Buber, Martin. The Knowledge of Man. London: G.
      Allen & Unwin, 1965. Buber never published his
      ideas about the unconscious, but in the introduction
      of this book Maurice Friedman claims to be working
      from notes taken while listening to Buber speak on
      the topic of the unconscious. Buber in general was
      very critical of any of what we can call the psycho-
      personal approaches regarding the unconscious.
      Buber would rather speak of an unconscious "between"
      people as the ground of relationship than about an un-
      conscious "in" people. As such, his understanding of
      the unconscious does not fit neatly with any of the
      four types mentioned.

92.   Bull, N. "Attitudes: conscious and unconscious."
      Journal of Nervous and Mental Disorders 103 (1946):
      337-45.

93.   Bundtzen, Lynda. "'Macbeth' and the rhetoric of the
      unconscious: an experiment in psychoanalytic criti-
      cism." Ph.D. dissertation, University of Chicago,
      1972. (Psycho-Personal Approach)

94.   Bunker, Henry A. "The unconscious." In Psychoanaly-
      sis and Social Work, edited by Marcel Heiman. New
      York: International Universities Press, 1953.
      (Psycho-Personal Approach)

95.   Burridge, W. "On the excitation processes of the con-
      scious and subconscious mind." Journal of Mental
      Science 75 (1929): 371-94. This article is a curious
      blend of experimentations with frog heart muscles,

nerve cells, and talk about conscious and subconscious activity. (Bio-Physical Approach)

96. Burton, A. "Death as a countertransference." Psycho-analysis and the Psychoanalytic Review 49, no. 4 (1962): 3-20. Burton, contrary to Freud, contends that the unconscious does know of death. (Psycho-Personal Approach)

97- Butler, Samuel. Unconscious Memory. New York:
98. E. P. Dutton and Company, 1924. In this book originally published in 1880, Butler discusses the ideas of Dr. Ewald Hering and those of Edward von Hartmann. The topics include memory, evolution, and subconsciousness.

99. Bzhalava, I. T. "K probleme bessoznatel'nogo v teorii ustanovki D. N. Uznadze." (The problem of the unconscious in D. N. Uznadze's theory of set.) Voprosy Psikhologii 13, no. 1 (1967): 155-59. Uznadze's theory is discussed and compared to Freudian ideas about the unconscious. (Psycho-Personal and Bio-Physical Approaches)

100. Caligor, Leopold. "The determination of the indivi-dual's unconscious conception of his own masculinity-femininity identification." Ph.D. dissertation, New York University, 1950. (Psycho-Personal Approach)

101. Callahan, Roger J. "Overcoming religious faith: A case history." Rational Living 2, no. 1 (1967): 16-21. It is contended that a person is not perma-nently influenced subconsciously by the religious upbringing one has had. (Psycho-Personal Approach)

102. Calwell, William. "The unconscious: A suggestion." Journal of Medical Science LXXI (1952): 97-100. The suggestion is that something called the "primi-tive brain" or "animal mind" in us is the physical basis of the unconscious. (Bio-Physical Approach)

103. Cargnello, Danilo. "Antropoanalisi e psicoanalisi." (Anthropoanalysis and psychoanalysis.) Archìvio Psicologia 10 (1949): 406-34. The differences be-tween anthropoanalysis (or Daseinsanalysis) and psychoanalysis are discussed. The article features a sixty-eight-item bibliography. Each school of

thought represents a distinct understanding of the unconscious. (Psycho-Personal Approach)

104. Carp, E. A. ["The problem of human confinement in connection with the nature of suggestion."] Neder-landsch tijdschrift voor psychologie 7 (1939): 235-59. The foundation of suggestion is discussed and, in the process, Carp uses such constructs as "collective unconscious" and "collective soul." (Transpersonal-Spiritual Approach)

105. Carus, Carl G. Psyche. New York: Spring Publication, 1970. This is a landmark work within the Romantic tradition regarding the unconscious. There is no doubt in reading Carus that the unconscious is something bigger-than-life. Indeed, the unconscious transcends as well as orchestrates all life processes. Carus distinguishes three aspects of the unconscious: the "Absolute Unconscious," the "Partial Absolute Unconscious," and the "Relative Unconscious." The book first appeared in 1846. (Transpersonal-Spiritual Approach)

106. Caruso, Igor A. "Sur la possibilité des influences positives de la psychanalyse sur la vie religieuse." (On the possibility of some positive influences of psychoanalysis on religious life.) Suppl. Vie Spirituel 11 (1958): 5-20. This is an argument for a psychology of the unconscious in the service of religious life, but argued in a reductionist mode. (Psycho-Personal Approach)

107. Castiglioni, Giulio. L'Inconscio. (The Unconscious.) Brescia: La Scuola, 1949.

108. Cayce, Hugh; Tom Clark; and Shane Miller. Dreams: The Language of the Unconscious. Virginia Beach: A. R. E. Press, 1967. (Psycho-Personal and Transpersonal-Spiritual Approaches)

109. Cesio, F. R. "On psychoanalytical technique: Evaluation of the basic 'here and now' conceptual formation of ideas of Freud on soothing the unconscious." Revista de Psicoanálisis 23, no. 2 (1966): 149-60. (Psycho-Personal Approach)

110. Chaffee, John H. "The psychoanalytic concept of the unconscious: A phenomenological critique." Ph.D.

dissertation, New York University, 1972. Chaffe argues that the Freudian notion of the unconscious is conceptually inadequate and presents an alternative view based on a phenomenological approach to account for certain behaviors. Explanations for behavior are not to be sought "behind" the behavior but "within" the behavior itself. (Psycho-Personal Approach)

111. Chambers, Jack A. "Beginning a multidimensional theory of creativity." Psychological Reports 25 (1969): 779-99. In the beginning of the article Chambers presents briefly various psychologies of the unconscious on the topic of creativity (Freud, Jung, Adler, and Rank). (Psycho-Personal and Transpersonal-Spiritual Approaches)

112. Chang, Pang-Ying V. "A Bayesian and information processing model of unconscious inference." Ph.D. dissertation, Wayne State University, 1975. (Bio-Physical and Psycho-Personal Approaches)

113. Charbonnier, G., and J. Granier. "La technique des images du Docteur Guillerey: Méthode psychothérapique." (Technique of images of Dr. Guillerey.) Evolution Psychiatrique 31, no. 4 (1966): 849-66. Image technique is presented as a road to the deeper layers of the unconscious. The technique involves a free association process. The relationship between this technique and Jung's method of active imagination is discussed. (Transpersonal-Spiritual Approach)

114. Chase, Harry W. "Psychoanalysis and the unconscious." Ph.D. dissertation, Clark University, 1910. (Psycho-Personal Approach)

115. Chertok, Leon. "The unconscious in France before Freud: Premises of a discovery." Psychoanalytic Quarterly 47, no. 2 (1978): 192-208. This is another "unconscious before Freud" account centering on the French medical and philosophical traditions before Freud. (Psycho-Personal Approach)

116. _____. "L'inconscient et l'hypnose." (The unconscious and hypnosis.) Annales médico-psychologiques 138, no. 5 (May 1980): 529-42. Chertok presents

both Soviet research on and psychoanalytical thinking
about the topic of the unconscious and hypnosis.
Chertok speculates about the psycho-physiological
dimensions of hypnosis and admits that we still know
very little about it. (Bio-Physical and Psycho-
Personal Approaches)

117. _____. "Reinstatement of the concept of the unconscious in the Soviet Union." American Journal of
Psychiatry 138, no. 5 (1981): 575-83. There is
a report on the symposium on the unconscious that
was held in Tbilisi, USSR in 1979. Chertok also
gives a review of Soviet psychology concerning the
unconscious. He discusses two opposing viewpoints;
that is, one view urging for an improved understanding of unconscious motivation, and the other
view maintaining the physiological orientated tradition of Pavlov. The article features many references. (Bio-Physical and Psycho-Personal
Approaches)

118. _____. "The unconscious and hypnosis." International Journal of Clinical Experimental Hypnosis.
30, no. 2 (Apr 1982): 95-107.

119. Chiba, Tanenari. "On the proper consciousness."
Psychologia 3 (1960): 65-72. The author is concerned about the possible misunderstandings surrounding the term "unconscious," and proposes a
new expression—"the proper consciousness."

120. Child, C. M. "The beginnings of unity and order in
living things." In The Unconscious, A Symposium,
pp. 11-42. Edited by C. M. Child. New York:
Alfred A. Knopf, 1927. Child reviews data from
experimental embryology on the basic properties of
protoplasm and on the significance of the environment for embryonic development. The point made
is that certain fundamental life processes are the
foundations of more complex functions. The
word "unconscious" is never mentioned. (Bio-
Physical Approach)

121. Chkhartishvili, Sh. N. Problema bessoznatel'nogo v
sovetskoi psikhologii. (Problem of the unconscious
in Soviet psychology.) Tbilisi, USSR: Metsniereba,
1966. The ideas of D. N. Uznadze are presented.

The point is made that conscious and unconscious are not distinct, separable categories, but are two aspects of one psychic structure. (Bio-Physical and Psycho-Personal Approaches)

122. Chyatte, C.; K. Mele; and B. Anderson. "Brain blood-shift theory: Verification of a predicted gradient in tactual-auditory rivalry." International Journal of Neuropsychiatry 3-4, no. 1 (1967-68): 360-64. It is suggested that repression is a result of the partial atrophy of unactivated neurons due to receiving low levels of blood nourishment. (Bio-Physical Approach)

123. Clapp, Chester D. "Two levels of unconscious awareness." Ph. D. dissertation, University of Michigan, 1952.

124. Clark, C. H. Brain-Storming. New York: Doubleday & Company, Inc., 1958. A notion of the subconscious is employed in explaining some of the processes involved in brain-storming.

125. Clark, James V. "A preliminary investigation of some unconscious assumptions affecting labor efficiency in eight supermarkets." Ph. D. dissertation, Harvard University, 1958. (Psycho-Personal Approach)

126. Cohen, E. D. "The collective unconscious and the universal forms." In C. G. Jung and the Scientific Attitude, Totowa, N. J.: Littlefield, Adams & Company, 1976. (Transpersonal-Spiritual Approach)

127. Cohen, S. Marc. "Incorrigibility, avowals and the concept of unconscious desire." Ph. D. dissertation, Cornell University, 1967. (Psycho-Personal Approach)

128. Collier, Rex. "A figure-ground model replacing the conscious-unconscious dichotomy." Journal of Individual Psychology 20 (1964): 3-16. Collier attempts to make a case for the autonomous individuality of the person by proposing a figure-ground model regarding how we are to understand the relationship between conscious and unconscious. The principle of continuity that is offered is ultimately based on the biological phenomena of gradients. (Psycho-Personal Approach)

129. Conkling, Mark. "Sartre's refutation of the Freudian unconscious." Review of Existential Psychology and Psychiatry 8, no. 2 (1968): 86-101. Sartre's views regarding the unconscious are presented as an alternative to the Freudian analytic toward the understanding of certain behaviors. See also Jean-Paul Sartre. (Psycho-Personal Approach)

130. _____. "Consciousness and the unconscious in William James' Principles of Psychology." Review of Existential Psychology and Psychiatry 11, no. 1 (1971): 25-42. Conkling presents the Jamesian position on the topic of unconscious mental states. James rejected the assumption of such states. See also William James. (Psycho-Personal Approach)

131. Conner, John W. "Projected image: The unconscious and the mass media." Journal of Psychoanalytic Anthropology 3, no. 4 (Fall 1980): 349-76. Interestingly the word "unconscious" is never used except in the title. The point is made that motion pictures give symbolic expression to the underlying hopes, fears, and anxieties of the age. (Socio-Cultural Approach)

132. Crampton, Michael. "Answers from the unconscious." Synthesis 1, no. 2 (1975): 140-52. The unconscious is presented as a vast storehouse of imagery that can be tapped into for answers to problems and inspiration. Crampton also issues some warnings in dealing with the unconscious. (Transpersonal-Spiritual Approach)

133. Cross, Pam W. "Intellectualizing about the value of the unconscious; or, unconscious resistance as a non-therapeutic technique." Perspectives in Psychiatric Care 14, no. 3 (1976): 130-32. (Psycho-Personal Approach)

134. Crown, Sidney. "Psychosomatics and the 'unconscious' mind-critique and evaluation." Journal of Psychosomatic Research 19, (1975): 307-18. In this philosophical-critical article Crown warns against what he calls "lazy reification" regarding the unconscious. He is in favor of operational models regarding the intervening processes between psychosocial stimulus and somatic responses. In fact, it is claimed that operational models within psycho-

somatic research have rendered the construct of
the unconscious superfluous.

135. Curtius, O. "Das kollektiv Unbewusste C. G. Jung,
seine Beziehung zur Personlichkeit und Gruppen-
seele." (The collective unconscious of Jung and its
relationship to the personality and the group soul.)
Zentralblatt für Psychotherapie 8 (1935): 265-79.
Curtius wrote this piece with a curious blend of
physiology and mysticism regarding the construct of
the collective unconscious.

136. Custer, Dan. The Miracle of Mindpower. Englewood
Cliffs, N.J.: Prentice-Hall, Inc., 1960. A notion
of the subconscious is used to account for the power
of the mind. (Transpersonal-Spiritual Approach)

137. Daim, Wilfried. Umwertung der Psychoanalyse.
(Transvaluation of psychoanalysis.) Vienna: Herold,
1951. The construct of the unconscious is discussed
from both a Freudian and Heideggerian perspective
with the intent of synthesizing the two. (Psycho-
Personal Approach)

138. D'Alessandro, Luigi. L'inconscio nella psicanalisi.
(Psychoanalysis and the unconscious.) Naples: Li-
breria Editrice Treves, 1958. (Psycho-Personal
Approach)

139. Dalton, Elizabeth C. "Unconscious structure in Dos-
toevsky's 'The Idiot': A study in literature and
and psychoanalysis." Ph.D. dissertation, Columbia
University, 1975. In this three-part study Dalton
discusses first how the novel itself has an unconscious expressed in form and content; second, the
oedipal and primal scene material of the novel; and
third, about tragic art as an expression of the death
instinct. (Psycho-Personal Approach)

140. Dalton, G. F. "Serialism and the unconscious." Journal of Social Psychology Research 37 (1954): 225-
35. This article features J. W. Dunne's theory of
serialism. Dalton presents what he calls a "geo-
graphy of the unconscious."

141. Danskin, David, and E. Dale Walter. "Biofeedback and
voluntary self-regulation: Counseling and education."

Personnel and Guidance Journal 51, no. 9 (1973): 633-38. This is a great piece of promotion literature for biofeedback. Regarding the unconscious the authors are contending that with and through biofeedback one can facilitate the surfacing of unconscious material. Biofeedback is suggested as another road to the unconscious. (Bio-Physical Approach)

142. Darnoi, Dennis N. "Eduard von Hartmann's metaphysics of the unconscious: A historical study and an evaluation on the basis of Aristotelian and Thomistic principles." Ph. D. dissertation, The Catholic University of America, 1964. In giving a critical expose of von Hartmann's principle of the unconscious Darnoi also makes a case against what he considers Hartmann's ideas represent; that is, moral nihilism, universal pessimism, and monistic pantheism. (Transpersonal-Spiritual Approach)

143. _____. The Unconscious and Eduard von Hartmann —A Historical-Critical Monograph. The Hague: Martinus Nijhoff, 1967. (Transpersonal-Spiritual Approach)

144. Davidson, Richard J. "On the psychobiology of attention and awareness: Scalp topography of averaged evoked responses to visual and auditory unconscious and conscious stimuli under varying attentional demands." Ph. D. dissertation, Harvard University, 1976. (Bio-Physical Approach)

145. De Andrade, Almir. "Uma análise da psicanálise à luz da fisiologia contemporâneas." (An analysis of psychoanalysis in the light of contemporary physiology.) Brazil Medicina 63 (1949): 103-11. It is argued that the Freudian unconscious is an unnecessary hypothesis and that it can be reduced to principles of neurophysiology and experimental psychology. (Bio-Physical Approach)

146. De Gaultier, J. "Le subconscient et les systèmes préhenseurs." (The subconscious and the apprehending system) La psychologie et la vie 3 (1929): 157-58. This article is about a book written by F. Paulhan entitled Les Puissances de l'Abstraction (The Powers of Abstraction).

147. de la Puente, Miguel. ["Consciousness and non-consciousness in Carl R. Rogers."] (In Portuguese). Arquivos Brasileiros de Psicologia 31, no. 3 (Jul-Sept 1979): 71-77. Rogerian ideas about the unconscious are presented and constrasted with those of Freud. (Psycho-Personal Approach)

148. Dendy, Helen. "Recent developments of the doctrine of subconscious process." Mind (1893): 371-73. This article was written to challenge what was then the tendency to break up the presumed unity of consciousness into a plurality of distinct sub-personalities or autonomous aspects of the psyche. (Psycho-Personal Approach)

149. De Neuter, Patrick. "L'inconscient: Le cas de l'homme aux rats comme commentaire clinique du texte metapsychologique." (The unconscious: The case of the Rat Man as a clinical commentary on the metapsychological text.) Revue de Psychologie et des Sciences de l'Education 6, no. 3 (1971): 275-92. The author attempts to clarify Freud's ideas concerning the unconscious. (Psycho-Personal Approach)

150. de Sanctis, S. "Istinto e incosciente." (Instinct and the unconscious.) Archîvio italiano di psicologia 5 (1926): 71-93. The ideas of W. H. R. Rivers are presented in relation to those of Freud and to the experiments of the English neurologist Head. (Bio-Physical and Psycho-Personal Approach)

151. de Silva, Manikku Wadu Padmasiri. "A study of motivational theory in early Buddhism with reference to the psychology of Freud." Ph.D. dissertation, University of Hawaii, 1967. It is argued that there is a concept of the unconscious in early Buddhism. The key concepts in Buddhism are "anusaya-s" (latent tendencies) and "asampajāna mano-sankhārā" (dispositions of the mind of which we are not aware). Although Buddhist analysis resembles somewhat the Freudian kind, it differs regarding methods of unravelling and mastering the unconscious. (Psycho-Personal Approach)

152. Desmond, S. Personality and Power. London: Templar Press, 1950. Desmond makes use of a notion

of the unconscious that is a source of personal
power. (Transpersonal-Spiritual Approach)

153. Dewhurst, David W. "The unconscious." Ph.D. dissertation, Cornell University, 1971. This is a pro-
Freudian thesis. Dewhurst makes a good point for
the basis in common sense of Freud's ideas. He
discusses at length the case of Dora to investigate
the question of unconscious motivation. He also
presents what he called the "Becket dilemma" to
discuss the question of proper motivation. (Psycho-
Personal Approach)

154. Didsbury. "Subconscient musical." (The musical subconscious.) Revista de Psicologia Aplicada 36
(1927): 72. The author discusses the role of the
subconscious in the creation of music.

155. Dietz, P. A. "Over onderbewuste voorkeur." (On
unconscious preference.) Nederlandsch tijdschrift
voor psychologie. It is argued that if subjects were
given the freedom to make any kind of selection
(for example, pick a color) they would reveal definite preferences rather than a chance distribution.
Dietz suggests that certain things have the same
symbolic value for many people. (Psycho-Personal
Approach)

156. Dilman, I. "The unconscious." Mind 68 (1959): 446-
73. The article deals exclusively with Freudian
terminology and thinking about the unconscious.
(Psycho-Personal Approach)

157. Dixon, Norman F. "The conscious/unconscious interface: Contributions to an understanding." Psychological Research Bulletin 21, no. 5 (1981). Several
theories of conscious/unconscious interface problems
are surveyed. A flow model is presented.

158. Dodds, E. R. The Greeks and the Irrational. Berkeley: University of California Press, 1951. Although Dodds does not deal with the topic of the
unconscious per se, this work is an excellent source
to trace the idea of the unconscious before the word
itself was coined. Indeed, the book could have
easily been entitled "The Greeks and the Unconscious." The unconscious is often considered the
source of irrational behavior and events.

159. Dongier, Maurice. "Observations neurobiologiques en relation avec les structures de l'inconscient." (Neurobiological observations in relationship to unconscious structures.) L'Evolution Psychiatrique 29, no. 2 (1964): 247-66. (Bio-Physical Approach)

160. Downing, George D. "Freud's concept of unconscious mind." Ph. D. dissertation, Yale University. 1969. (Psycho-Personal Approach)

161. Drach, Margaret. "Creativity, competence, and the unconscious: Aspects of Chomsky and Lévi-Strauss." Ph. D. dissertation, Harvard University, 1978.

162. Drews, A. "Das Unbewusste in de Philosphie und Psychoanalyse." (The unconscious in philosophy and and psychoanalysis.) Philosophie und Leben 5 (1929): 341-59. (Psycho-Personal Approach).

163. Drews, J. "Ein Kratersturz ins Unbewusste. Zur Konstruktion von Traum and Tagtraum Arno Schmidts Roman 'Kaff Auch Mare Crisium'." (Plunge into the unconscious. Construction of dreams and day dreams in Arno Schmidt's novel, "Kaff auch mare Crisium.") Psyche 35, no. 12 (Dec 1981): 1103-21.

164. Dreyfuss, C. "Le suicide inconscient." (Unconscious suicide.) Ther Umsch 37, no. 1 (Jan 1980): 17-22. (Psycho-Personal Approach)

165. Drobec, E., and H. Strotzka. "Narkodiagnostische Untersuchungen bei Surrealisten." (Narcoanalyses of surrealists.) Zeitschrift für Psychotherapie und medizinische Psychologie 1 (1951): 64-71. The unconscious as the source of creativity is the topic here. Two surrealist artists were interviewed under narcosis.

166. Dummer, E. S. "Introduction." In The Unconscious, A Symposium, pp. 1-10. Edited by C. M. Child. New York: Alfred A. Knopf, 1927. Dummer presents the purpose of the symposium, which was to gather ideas representing different sciences and diverse points of view regarding the integrative action of the unconscious relative to cognitive processes.

167. Dunlap. "Consciousness, the unconscious, and mysticism." Philosophical Review 37 (1928): 72-74.

168. Dwelschauvers, G. "Freud et la psychanalyse." (Freud and psychoanalysis.) Revue de philosophie 34 (1927): 7-23, 153-67. The author is very critical of Freudian psychoanalysis. He considers it to be inconsistent and unscientific. Dwelschauvers considers the Freudian unconscious to be a mysterious force because it is not merely related to one's personal history.

169. _____. "Les activités subconscientes et leur utilisation." (Subconscious activities and their utilization.) La psychologie et la vie 6 (1932): 6-12. The author is trying to explain how the phenomenon of invention occurs. In doing so he distinguishes two classes of subconscious processes: dynamic subconscious ones and automatic subconscious ones. Some of these processes can be trained to facilitate the activity of invention.

170. Ebbers, H. "Beiträge zum Problem des Unbewussten und der psychischen Realität." (Concerning the problem of the unconscious and of psychical reality.) Archiv für die gesamte Psychologie 87 (1933): 69-128. Ebbers writes about five strata of unconsciousness. All these levels are somehow influenced by consciousness, hence no level is absolutely independent. (Psycho-Personal Approach)

171. Eccles, John C. The Human Mystery. New York: Springer International, 1979. The entire book is devoted to brain research. What is relevant to the topic of the unconscious is that section wherein Eccles discusses the right, nondominant hemisphere as being related to the unconscious. (Bio-Physical Approach)

172. Edel, Abraham. "The concept of the unconscious: Some analytic preliminaries." Philosophy of Science 31, no. 1 (1964): 18-33. Eleven questions are distinguished that relate to the philosophical discussion of the unconscious. The questions involve such things as logic, linguistics, methodology, metaphysics, to name a few. Edel offers these questions

as a way to help clarify some of the issues surrounding the construct of the unconscious. The article is excellent for references.

173. Edinger, Edward F. "The collective unconscious as manifested in psychosis." American Journal of Psychotherapy 9 (1955): 624-29. A Jungian framework is assumed in this discussion of archetypes and their relationship to psychotic delusions. (Transpersonal-Spiritual Approach)

174. _____. "Metaphysics and the unconscious." In Ego and Archetype. New York: Putnam, 1972. Edinger discusses with examples how sometimes the unconscious can enlighten an unphilosophical person regarding the mystery of being. A Jungian framework is assumed here. (Transpersonal-Spiritual Approach)

175. Eecke, Wilfried Ver. "Of Freud's theory of negation." Man and World 14 (1981): 111-25. Eecke is arguing for an alternative position vis-à-vis Freud's contention that patients sometimes lie about their conditions, and Sartre's contention that patients simply do not want to know the truth about their situation. Eecke is suggesting that it is also possible that patients simply have limits to their ability to achieve greater self-knowledge.

176. Ehrenzweig, Anton. The Psycho-Analysis of Artistic Vision and Hearing. London: Routledge & Paul, 1953. The topics here include the subconscious, music, art, and perception. (See also item no. 581)

177. Eidelberg, Ludwig. "The concept of the unconscious." Psychiatric Quarterly 27 (1953): 563-87. Basically this is a straightforward, point-by-point exposé of Freudian psychology and, as such, a good introduction to Freud. (Psycho-Personal Approach)

178. Eissler, K. P. "Freud and the psychoanalysis of history." Journal of the American Psychoanalytic Association 11, no. 4 (1963): 675-703. The author uses Japanese history to illustrate the importance of understanding unconscious factors in the history of peoples.

179. Eliasberg, W. "The absolute and the unconscious."
Journal of Nervous and Mental Disease 100 (1944):
44-48. This is a rather dated and strange anti-
Freudian piece of writing. The real topic of discussion seems to be the relationship between Freudian ideas and America.

180. _____. "Early criticism of Freud's psychoanalysis."
Psychoanalytic Review 41 (1954): 347-53. It is
argued that much of the criticism leveled against
the existence of the unconscious came from those
who prided themselves on the role and rule of consciousness. (Psycho-Personal Approach)

181. Elkin, Henry. "The unconscious and the integration of
personality." Review of Existential Psychology and
Psychiatry 5, no. 2 (1965): 176-89. The article
is devoted primarily to object-relations theory. In
one place Elkin suggests that Jung's construct of the
collective unconscious really has to do with the in-
fant's experiences in about the first eighteen months
of life. In short, with Elkin the transpersonal dimension of the collective unconscious collapses into
the psycho-personal.

182. Ellenberger, Henri. "The unconscious before Freud."
Bulletin of the Menninger Clinic 21, no. 3 (1957).
In this article, short but packed with historical
references, Ellenberger outlines five types of unconsciouses. The five include the metaphysical
unconscious, the biological unconscious, the deep
psychological unconscious, the more accessible
psychological unconscious, and the dynamic unconscious of Freud.

183. _____. The Discovery of the Unconscious. New
York: Basic Books, Inc., 1970. Despite the title
the book really has more to do with the history of
the central figures of psychiatry. There are,
though, some short sections that deal explicitly with
the topic of the unconscious. This is an excellent
historical source.

184. Engelhardt, Tristram H., and Stuart Spicker, eds.
"Luminosity: The unconscious in the integrated
person." In Mental Health: Philosophical Perspectives, pp. 177-89. Dordrecht: Reidel, 1978.

185. Epstein, Arthur. "Dream formation during an epileptic seizure: Implications for the study of the 'unconscious'." Journal of American Academy of Psychoanalysis 5, no. 1 (1977): 43-49. Epstein has his own way of understanding what the unconscious is. For him it refers to what he called the "dreaming mind." (Psycho-Personal Approach)

186. Epstein, Seymour. "Conscious and unconscious self-evaluation in a schizophrenic and control group." Ph.D. dissertation, University of Wisconsin, 1953. (Psycho-Personal Approach)

187. Erdheim, M. "Freud's Grossenphantasien, sein Konzept des Unbewussten und die Wiener Decadence." (Freud's delusions of grandeur, his concept of the unconscious and the Vienna decadence.) Psyche 35, no. 10 (Oct 1981): 857-74. (Psycho-Personal Approach)

188. _____. "Freud's Grossenphantasien, sein Konzept des Unbewussten und die Wiener Decadence (II)." (Freud's fantasies of grandeur, his concept of the unconscious, and Viennese decadence, part II.) Psyche 35, no. 11 (Nov 1981): 1006-33.

189. Erickson, M. "The experimental demonstration of unconscious mentation by automatic writing." Psychoanalytic Quarterly 6 (1937): 513-29. This article features two so-called experiments (really episodes) involving hypnotism and automatic writing. It is suggested that the unconscious is an entity that can make intentions known through automatic writing.

190. Evans, Richard I. Conversations with Carl Jung and Reactions from Ernest Jones. Princeton, N. J.: Van Nostrand, 1964. The focus is on the topic of personality development with Jung and Jones offering their views. The nature and role of the unconscious is discussed vis-à-vis personality development.

191. Ey, H., ed. L'Inconscient. (The Unconscious.) Bruges, Belgium: Descles de Brouwer, 1966. The unconscious is discussed in relation to drives (according to Lebovici and Diatkine), linguistics (Laplanche and Leclaire), neurophysiology (Blanc), psychiatric problems (Ey), and philosophical thought (DeWaelhaeas).

192. Fairchild, R. W. "Pastor, meet Dr. Jung." Pacific
      Theological Review (Win 1975). This is an exercise
      in the psychology of the unconscious and religion.
      (Transpersonal-Spiritual Approach)

193. Farrell, B. A. "Can psychoanalysis be refuted?" In-
      quiry 3-4 (1960-61): 16-35, 46-51. In reference
      to the unconscious Farrell discusses the noun and
      adjectival usages of the word by Freud. (Psycho-
      Personal Approach)

194. Fast, J. "A new signal from the unconscious." In
      Body Language, pp. 2-3. New York: Pocket Books,
      1970. This book is interesting and informative
      about body language, but careless theoretically re-
      garding the use of the noun form of the word "un-
      conscious." Fast implies that the unconscious in us
      is responsible for sending and receiving body mes-
      sages. However, he is really referring to the sub-
      tle autonomic patterns of responses that usually ac-
      company psychological states. (Bio-Physical Ap-
      proach)

195. Favez-Boutonier, J. "L'activité volontaire." (Volun-
      tary activity.) Bulletin de Psychologie 18, no.
      16/240 (1965): 913-16. The author presents P.
      Ricoeur's ideas about the Freudian unconscious and
      will. Also there is a discussion of Guillame's ideas
      about habits and instincts.

196. Feibleman, James. "The rational unconscious."
      Journal of General Psychology 52 (1955): 157-62.
      Feibleman contrasts the emotional unconscious (à la
      Freud) with what he called the "rational uncon-
      scious." The latter is at work in discovery, inven-
      tion, and in induction. (Psycho-Personal Approach)

197. Felber, Stanislav. Vedomie a podvedomie. (Conscious-
      ness and subconsciousness.) Bratislava: Slovenská
      Akadémia Vied a Umeni, 1948. Felber conducts a
      materialist (Marxist) attack on psychoanalysis. He
      explains all mental phenomena, conscious and uncon-
      scious, to be essentially a matter of physiological
      processes. The mind is determined by such factors
      as heredity, conditioned reflexes, and the environ-
      ment. (Bio-Physical Approach)

198. Feldman, A. Bronson. The Unconscious in History.
      New York: Philosophical Library, 1959. The au-
      thor is working within the psychoanalytic framework.

199. Feldman, Jeffrey B. "The utilization of the subliminal
      psychodynamic activation method in the further ex-
      amination of conscious and unconscious measures of
      death anxiety. " Ph. D. dissertation, Case Western
      Reserve University, 1978.

200. Feldstein, Leonard. Choros: The Orchestrating Self.
      New York: Fordham University Press, 1984. This
      book features Feldstein's own writings on the uncon-
      scious. (Transpersonal-Spiritual Approach)

201. Ferrari, G. C. "Gli elementi subcoscienti nella fatica
      industriale. " (The subconscious elements in indus-
      trial work.) Rivista di psicologia 27 (1931): 153-
      60.

202. Ferrière, A. Education religieuse et psychologie de
      l'inconscient. (Religious education and psychology
      of the unconscious.) Geneva: Labor et Fides,
      1951. Ferrière distinguishes twelve levels of per-
      sonality development and discusses the psychological
      types that relate to each level.

203. Field, G. C. "Is the conception of the unconscious of
      value in psychology?" Mind 31 (1922): 414-23.
      It is argued that at best the construct of the uncon-
      scious is an x-factor. It does not represent a real
      advance in our knowledge of human behavior. Field
      rejects the implications that the unconscious is a
      "thing. " This piece represents one third of a
      three-part discussion on the topic. See also F.
      Aveling and J. Laird.

204. Filliozat, Jean. "L'inconscient dans la psychologie in-
      dienne. " (The unconscious in the Indian psychology.)
      Proceeds of the 10th International Congress of Phil-
      osophy (1948-49): 267-69. This article features a
      comparison between yogic notions, such as "sam-
      skara, " with ideas set forth by Janet, Prince, and
      psychoanalysis. (Psycho-Personal Approach)

205. Filloux, Jean. L'inconscient. (The unconscious.)
      Paris: Presses Universitaires de France, 1947.
      Drawing heavily upon French history Filloux wrote

another "unconscious before Freud." The book also
features a discussion of the TAT and the Rorschach
Test as therapeutic tools, and the Freudian influences
on art and literature (particularly French).

206. Fingarette, H. "'Unconscious behavior' and allied concepts: A new approach to their empirical interpretation." The Journal of Philosophy XLVII, no. 18
(Aug 31, 1950).

207. Fischer, W. "The problem of unconscious motivation."
Humanitas 3, no. 3 (1968): 259-72. Fischer includes a good summary of Freud's three ways of
using the term "unconscious"; that is, as a descriptive adjective, as a referrent for a place, and as a
term implying a dynamic sense. Besides the unconscious he also discusses motivation, tribe, and instincts. (Psycho-Personal Approach)

208. Fisher, John B. "Reasons, causes and the unconscious
in Freud." Ph.D. dissertation, City University of
New York, 1977. This is a philosophical-critical
study of the models of explanation presupposed by
Freud's theory of unconscious motivation. The
reason-giving model and the causal model are distinguished and discussed. (Psycho-Personal Approach)

209. Fitch, Stanley K. Insights into Human Behavior. Boston: Holbrook, 1974. The author discusses the
importance of the unconscious toward understanding
human behavior. He also discusses the correlation
between animal and human behavior.

210. Flew, A. "Motives and the unconscious." In Minnesota
studies in the philosophy of science. Vol I. The
foundations of science and the concepts of psychology
and psychoanalysis, pp. 155-73. Edited by Herbert
Feigl and Michael Scriven. Minneapolis: University of Minnesota Press, 1956. (Psycho-Personal
Approach)

211. Foote, Theodore. The Source of Power. Baltimore:
Williams & Wilkins Company, 1922. Foote makes
use of a notion of the subconscious as the source
of power. (Transpersonal-Spiritual Approach)

212. Fordham, Michael. Objective Psyche. London: Rout-
     ledge & Kegan Paul, Ltd., 1958. The Jungian
     construct of the Objective Psyche, also known as
     the Collective Unconscious, is discussed.
     (Transpersonal-Spiritual Approach)

213. Forgus, R. H. "Subception and subliminal event." In
     Perception, pp. 259-67. New York: McGraw-Hill,
     1966. The construct of the unconscious is rejected
     in favor of understanding certain behaviors in terms
     of physiological factors. (Bio-Physical Approach)

214. Fornari, Franco. "La psicoanalisi della guerra."
     (Psychoanalysis of war.) Rivista di Psicoanalisi
     10, no. 3 (1964): 209-89. The author discusses
     the unconscious processes at work in war and indi-
     vidual responsibility. (Psycho-Personal and Socio-
     Cultural Approaches)

215. Fox, Michael A. "Explanation and the unconscious."
     Ph.D. dissertation, University of Toronto, 1970.
     Fox wrote much of this in response to A. MacIn-
     tyre's monograph, which argued that Freud's hypo-
     thesis of the unconscious, although acceptable, was
     not truly explanatory. Fox argues that it is expla-
     natory in the fullest sense. See also A. MacIntyre.
     (Psycho-Personal Approach)

216. _____. "Unconscious emotions: A reply to Pro-
     fessor Mullane." Philosophy and Phenomenological
     Research 36, no. 3 (1976): 412-14. (Psycho-
     Personal Approach)

217. Frankenstein, C. "Bishelat habilti muda." (On the
     unconscious.) Iyyun 4 (1953): 133-48. The author
     discusses the following connotations of the uncon-
     scious that have shaped modern depth psychology of
     the unconscious: 1) the unconscious as a modality
     of psychic contents; 2) the unconscious as a part of
     the psychic structure; 3) the unconscious as a sum
     of constituents of experience; and 4) the unconscious
     as a force of life, a creative source.

218. Frankl, Victor. The Unconscious God. New York:
     Simon and Schuster, 1975. Frankl makes use of
     the expressions "instinctual unconscious," "spiritual
     unconscious," and "transcendent unconscious." He

contends that just as the instincts (sex and aggres-
sion) if denied will somehow erupt into consciousness and behavior, so too the so-called "spiritual"
instincts will break through if denied. He also
writes that a person is always in a relationship
with the Transcendent Thou via the unconscious.
(Transpersonal-Spiritual Approach)

219. Frayn, R. S. Revelation and the Unconscious. London:
      Epworth Press, 1940. The unconscious is distin-
      guished according to two aspects. The unconscious
      is understood as the psychic refuse of consciousness;
      but in its deepest layer the unconscious is consi-
      dered to be in direct contact with divinity, hence the
      ability to receive revelations. (Transpersonal-
      Spiritual Approach)

220. Freeman, R. Unconscious Witness. New York: Dodd,
      Mead, 1942.

221. Frenkel-Brunswik, Else. "Meaning of psychoanalytic
      concepts and confirmation of psychoanalytic theo-
      ries." Science Monthly 79 (1954): 293-300. It is
      argued that the Freudian system of ideas is within
      the framework of scientific concepts and methods.
      The construct of the unconscious is presented as a
      case in point. Other concepts are also discussed.
      (Psycho-Personal Approach)

222. Freud, Sigmund. Everything Freud wrote and virtually
      everything written about Freud and his ideas have
      some relevance to the topic of the unconscious.
      Listing all these references would require a sepa-
      rate bibliography and one far lengthier than this one.
      For the sake of economy we will refer to the Ab-
      stracts of the Standard Edition of the Complete
      Psychological Works of Sigmund Freud, edited by
      Carrie L. Rothgeb and published by the U. S. Gov-
      ernment Printing Office in 1971. The intention is
      to use the Abstracts under the entry "Unconscious,"
      and to list the references therein. In this way one
      would have the initial, major references in the
      Freudian corpus regarding the topic of the uncon-
      scious. In the end some other references, not in
      the corpus, will be cited. Virtually everything
      written by Freud can be subsumed within the Psycho-
      Personal Approach.

223-   . "Papers on metapsychology. The unconscious.
33.   Appendix A: Freud and Ewald Hering. Appendix B:
        Psycho-physical parallelism. Appendix C: Words
        and things." Vol. 14.

234.   . "Studies on hysteria. Unconscious ideas and
        ideas inadmissible to consciousness—splitting of
        the mind." Vol. 2.

235.   . "The interpretation of dreams. The psycho-
        logy of the dream processes. The unconscious and
        consciousness—reality." In this work Freud intro-
        duces his topographic model of the psyche employing
        the expressions "conscious," "preconscious," and
        "unconscious." Vol. 5.

236.   . "Jokes and their relation to the unconscious."
        Vol. 8.

237.   . "Delusions and dreams in Jensen's Gradiva.
        Gradiva and the psychology of the unconscious."
        Vol. 9.

238.   . "A note on the unconscious in psychoanaly-
        sis." Vol. 12.

239.   . "Papers on metapsychology. The Uncon-
        scious." Vol. 14. It is here that Freud continues
        his exposition of the topographic model of the psyche.
        It was first introduced in his "Interpretation of
        Dreams."

240.   . "Introductory lectures on psychoanalysis.
        General theory of the neuroses. Fixation to trau-
        mas—The unconscious." Vol. 16.

241.   . "The ego and the id. Consciousness and
        what is unconscious." Vol. 19. Here Freud presents
        the structural model of the psyche using the expres-
        sions "Id," "Ego," and "Superego."

242.   . On Creativity and the Unconscious. Papers
        by Freud on the psychology of Art, Literature and
        Religion, selected by Benjamin Nelson. New York:
        Harper & Row, 1958. (Psycho-Personal Approach)

243. Frey, E. "Zur Biologie der Gefühisdynamik und Sym-
        bolbildung." (Biology of the dynamics of feeling

and symbol formation.) Schweizer Archiv für Neurologie un Psychiatrie 50 (1942): 74-87. Frey discusses the unconscious in relation to symbol formation, and to what he referred to as "cosmic instincts."

244-
45.
Frey-Rohn, Lilliane. From Freud to Jung. A Comparative Study of the Psychology of the Unconscious. New York: Delta Books, 1974. Freud and Jung are compared and constrasted from the viewpoint of a Jungian. See E. Glover for the same type of work done from the viewpoint of a Freudian.

246. Friederici. "Heilpädagogik und Tiefenpsychologie." (Curative pedagogy and psychology of the unconscious.) Hilfsschule 21 (1928): 418-22. It is contended that psychoanalytic education can help to free the child of complexes, that analysis of the teacher is important, and that all teachers should understand the psychology of the unconscious as well as parapsychology. Friederici considers suggestion and hypnosis two second important fields of the psychology of the unconscious. (Psycho-Personal Approach)

247. Friedmann, M. "Die Überlastung des Unbewussten in der Psychoanalyse." (The overburdening of the unconscious in psychoanalysis.) Allgemeine ärztliche Zeitschrift für Psychotherapie und psychische Hygiene 1 (1928): 65-86. The status of various Freudian terms are assessed. It is argued that the construct of the unconscious continues to be necessary for psychoanalysis. (Psycho-Personal Approach)

248. Friedman, Maurice. "The changing image of human nature: Philosophical aspect." American Journal of Psychoanalysis 26-27 (1966-67): 138-47. Regarding the topic of the unconscious Friedman made these points: 1) the psychology of the unconscious has introduced us to the consideration of unconscious motivation; 2) the reality of unconscious compulsion challenges us again to answer the question of free will or determinism; and 3) the unmasking process of searching for hidden motivation, although in the service of truth, ultimately and ironically renders all truth questionable. (Psycho-Personal Approach)

249. Froeschels, Emil. "About the name and some patho-
logic functions of the 'unconscious'." Journal of
Clinical Psychopathology and Psychotherapy 7 (1945):
273-79. Froeschels offers to substitute the expressions "expression-ripe" for "conscious," "nearly-
expression-ripe" for "preconscious," and "not-
expression-ripe" for "unconscious." It is contended
that these newer expressions can be better defined.
It seems though that Froeschels is assuming a
Freudian understanding of the unconscious but in a
new verbal dress. (Psycho-Personal Approach)

250. Fromm, Erich. Psychoanalysis and Religion. New
Haven, Conn.: Yale University Press, 1950. In
one section Fromm distinguishes his concept of
the unconscious with that of Freud and Jung.
Fromm considers Freud's negative view of the unconscious and Jung's positive view of it to be one-
sided distortions. Fromm sees the unconscious in
more neutral terms; that is, as something that one
does not necessarily fear or hold in awe. It is
simply the excluded aspect that ought to be integrated with the organized ego. (Psycho-Personal Approach)

251. _____. The Forgotten Language. New York: Holt,
Rinehart, and Winston, 1951. Fromm makes it
clear that he does not see the unconscious as a
distinct category, as something that is more or less
permanently there. He understands the unconscious
in relative terms. For example, the day world can
be considered the unconscious of the sleep-dream
world and vice versa. (Psycho-Personal Approach)

252. _____. Zen Buddhism and Psychoanalysis. New
York: Harper and Brothers, 1960. Here we have
an interface between a psychology of the unconscious
and the Zen worldview. D. T. Suzuki contributed
an article relating the unconscious with psychoanalysis. See D. T. Suzuki.

253. Frosch, J. "The role of unconscious homosexuality in
the paranoid constellation." Psychoanalytic Quarterly 50, no. 4 (1981): 587-613. Frosch reviews the
literature dealing with Freud's views on the topic.
(Psycho-Personal Approach)

254. Fuhrer, M. J., and C. W. Eriksen. "The unconscious
     perception of the meaning of verbal stimuli." Jour-
     nal of Abnormal Social Psychology 61 (1960): 432-
     39. This experimental study found no evidence for
     unconscious perception. (Bio-Physical Approach)

255. Gabriel, Y. "The fate of the unconscious in the human
     sciences." Psychoanalytic Quarterly 51, no. 2
     (Apr 1982): 246-83. This is a pro-Freudian piece
     wherein Gabriel answers some of the criticisms of
     Freud's central concepts. It is contended that the
     concept of the unconscious is an indispensable as-
     sumption. (Psycho-Personal Approach)

256. Gaito, John. "Stages of perception, unconscious pro-
     cesses, and information extraction." Journal of
     General Psychology 70, no. 1 (1964): 183-97.

257. Galin, David. "Implications for psychiatry of left and
     right cerebral specialization." Archives of General
     Psychiatry 31 (Oct 1974): 572-83. Galin argues
     that the right, nondominant hemisphere could be the
     anatomical locus for the unconscious. He points
     out that the right hemisphere's mode of thought is
     similar to Freud's description of the unconscious.
     (Bio-Physical Approach)

258. Gallwey, W. Timothy. The Inner Game of Tennis.
     New York: Bantam Books, 1974. For the most
     part this is a book about tennis. Gallwey embel-
     lishes the book with talk about the "unconscious
     mind" and "Self #2 and #3" as key factors in good
     tennis playing. What he attributes to the uncon-
     scious mind others would say was simply a case of
     automatism. (Transpersonal-Spiritual Approach)

259. Garnett, A. C. Instinct and Personality. New York:
     Dodd, Mead, 1928. The author discusses theories
     of instincts such as that of McDougall and ideas
     about the unconscious such as those of Freud and
     Prince. Garnett is arguing for the supremacy of
     the "urge" or "horme" in all behavior. (Bio-
     Physical and Psycho-Personal Approaches)

260. Gauss, C. E. "The theoretical backgrounds of surreal-
     ism." Journal of Aesthetics 2, no. 8 (1943): 37-44.

Gauss discusses the relationship between surrealism and Jung's theory of the collective unconscious. (Transpersonal-Spiritual Approach)

261. Geiger, M. Fragment über den Begriff des Unbewussten und die psychische Realität. (Fragment on the
concept of the unconscious and psychic reality.)
Halle: Niemeyer, 1930.

262. Geley, Gustave. L'être Subconscient. (The Subconscious Being.) Paris: F. Alcan, 1926.
(Transpersonal-Spiritual Approach)

263. _____. From the Unconscious to the Conscious.
New York: Harper & Brothers Publishers, 1920.
Geley announced that this book is the sequel to his
other book The Subconscious Being. Geley follows
the tradition of Carus and Hartmann in understanding
the unconscious to be bigger-than-life and indeed the
very source and director of life. It seems that in
this book Geley is arguing a theory of the unconscious to account for evolution. (Transpersonal-
Spiritual Approach)

264. Gerson, M. "Hapsihoanaliza l'or hamarxism." (Psychoanalysis in the light of Marxism.) Ofakim 8
(1954): 133-39. This is a rare case where a Marxist
affirms some of Freud's clinical concepts, such as
the unconscious, repression, and so forth. Gerson
has difficulties, though, with Freud's sociological
interpretations. (Psycho-Personal Approach)

265. Gil, Daniel. ["The unconscious: The shattering of discourse, discourse of the shattering."] (In Spanish.)
Revista Uruguaya de Psicoanálisis no. 57 (Jan 1978):
59-86. This is a discussion of language and the
Freudian unconscious. There are some references
to J. Lacan. (Psycho-Personal Approach)

266. Gil, M. Psychological Issues. Vol. III, no. 2, monograph 10. New York: International Universities
Press, Inc., 1963. Gil discusses the three ways
the expression "unconscious" is used; that is, as a
descriptive adjective of all that is not conscious,
in the dynamic sense referring to all that is kept
repressed, and in the systematic sense alluding to
a system of impulses, drives, and so forth.
(Psycho-Personal Approach)

267. Gillibert, Jean. "Fantasme inconscient et phantasme de l'inconscient." (Unconscious fantasy and fantasy of the unconscious.) Revue Française de Psycho-analyse 35, no. 2-3 (Mar 1971): 253-76. The ideas of Freud, Klein, and Kant are discussed in regard to the power of fantasization. A clinical case is cited. (Psycho-Personal Approach)

268. Glover, Edward. "Unbewusste Wünsche im Alltagsleben." (Unconscious wishes in daily life.) Psychologie Bewegung 5 (1933): 485-500. This is Glover's speech to the London Institute of Psychoanalysis. He covers such topics as unconscious automatisms, influences of wishes, sublimation, and projection. (Psycho-Personal Approach)

269. _____. Freud or Jung. London: George Allen & Unwin, 1950. Freud and Jung are compared and contrasted from the point of view of a Freudian. See L. Frey-Rohn for a similar work done by a Jungian. In both books two psychologies of the unconscious are contrasted and compared.

270. Gnepp, E. "The psychology of man: A general theory." Psychology 10, no. 3 (1973): 21-34. Gnapp turns the tables on both classical and behaviorist thinking by contending that the unconscious is rational and that consciousness is responsible for irrationality.

271. Goitein, P. "The lady from the sea." Psychoanalytic Review 14 (1927): 375-419. Goitein conducts a Freudian analysis of one of Ibsen's dramas. In it, Goitein contends that Fate symbolizes the unconscious. (Psycho-Personal Approach)

272. Goldberg, Hillel. "An early psychologist of the unconscious." Journal of the History of Ideas XLIII, no. 2 (Apr-Jun 1982): 269-84. Goldberg writes about Israel Salanter (1810-1883), an East European rabbi. Goldberg attempts to show that Salanter expounded a distinct theory of the unconscious, along Freudian lines, but before Freud. (Psycho-Personal Approach)

273. Goldiamond, I. "Indicators of perception: I. Subliminal perception, subception, unconscious perception:

An analysis in terms of psychophysical indicator methodology." Psychological Bulletin 55, no. 6 (1958): 373-411. Literature pertaining to unconscious processes in perception is reviewed with the intent of updating and relating the findings to psychophysical indicator methodology. One hundred and ninety-eight references are cited. (Bio-Physical Approach)

274. Goldman, Norman. "Rabbinic theology and the unconscious." Journal of Religion and Health 17, no. 2 (1978): 144-50. Goldman argues in favor of incorporating a psychology of the unconscious within rabbinic counseling. He also presents and discusses those places where Jewish theology and the psychology of the unconscious interface such as centering on the notions of "Shekinah" and "Yezer-ha-rah."

275. _____. "An investigation into a rabbinic understanding of 'Yezer-ha-rah' and the unconscious." D. Min. dissertation, Eastern Baptist Theological Seminary, 1980. Here Goldman presents the expanded version of his ideas that were mentioned in the entry above. When he speaks of the unconscious in relation to "Shekinah" (Divine presence) he is using a transpersonal-spiritual approach. When he speaks of it in terms of "Yezer-ha-rah" (the evil principle in us) he is working with a psycho-personal approach regarding the unconscious.

276. Goldstein, Melvin. "Film as a cultural mirror of the unconscious of the masses." Journal of Psychohistory 5, no. 3 (Win 1978): 443-52. Goldstein reviews Paul Monaco's work Cinema and Society: France and Germany During the Twenties. The point made is that motion pictures have a certain wish fulfillment, fantasy releasing, and cathartic value for the masses. (Socio-Cultural Approach)

277. González-Bustamante, Juan José. "La problemática de la culpa y la sociedad." (The problem of penal guilt and society.) Revista Mexicana de Sociologia 13 (1951): 63-82. The author stresses the point that the unconscious needs to be considered when dealing with penal guilt. (Psycho-Personal Approach)

278. Gordon, W. J. "Conscious/subconscious interaction in a creative act." Journal of Creative Behavior 15, no. 1 (1981): 1-10.

279. Gould, Nathan. "The structure of dialectical reason: A comparative study of Freud's and Lévi-Strauss' concept of unconscious mind." Ethos 6, no. 4 (1978): 187-211. Gould argues that there is an affinity between Lévi-Strauss' notion of unconscious mind ("esprit") and Freud's ideas concerning the unconscious aspects of the ego. Both, according to Gould, have to do with the unconsciousness of certain rational-cognitive processes. (Psycho-Personal Approach)

280. Grabe, Erna F. The Sub-Conscious Speaks. Los Angeles: DeVorss, 1932. (Transpersonal-Spiritual Approach)

281. Granone, F. "Stati di coscienza in ipnosi." (Conscious states in hypnosis.) Rassegna Italiana di Ricerca Psichica 1 (1966): 35-40. Granone distinguishes such concepts as self-awareness, subconscious, biological unconscious, and psychic unconscious in order to better understand certain hypnotic events.

282. Gras, V. W. "Myth and the reconciliation of opposites: Jung and Lévi-Strauss." Journal of the History of Ideas XLII, no. 3 (Jul-Sept 1981): 471-87. It is contended that both Jung and Lévi-Strauss are guilty of wanting to establish an Archimedean point outside history in order to legitimize their systems of ideas. Gras maintains that the "natural psyche" or "collective unconscious" that they theorize about does not exist universally in nature but historically in culture. In other words, it was not discovered but created.

283. Greenberg, H. R. "Psychiatry and the Arts." In Comprehensive Textbook of Psychiatry/III, pp. 3121-3129. Edited by H. Kaplan, A. Freedman, and B. Sadock. Baltimore: William & Wilkins, 1980. Here we have an interface between a psychology of the unconscious (Freudian) and the creative process.

284. Greenleaf, Eric. "The 'unconscious mind mirror' in active imagination." Psychotherapy: Theory, Re-

search, and Practice 12, no. 2 (1975): 202-6.
Greenleaf offers another "royal road to the unconscious." With this technique one imagines a mirror and one's image in it. Then with eyes closed
one is to step back, open one's eyes and see the
unconscious mind's image of oneself. (Psycho-
Personal Approach). See also Loren Pedersen.

285. Gregory, Joshua. "The concept of mind and the unconscious." British Journal of the Philosophy of
Science 2 (1951): 52-57. Gregory criticizes Ryle,
who criticized the Cartesian doctrine of mind.
Gregory argues that Ryle underestimated the elabor-
ate organization of the unconscious and thereby ignored the complex nature of causation. (Psycho-
Personal Approach)

286. Groddeck, George. The Book of the It. New York:
Funk & Wagnalls, 1950. The "It" or the "Unknown
Self" works behind the scenes of our lives and di-
rects our lives. It is not the unconscious in the
Freudian sense, but one more in accord with the
transpersonal-spiritual approach.

287. _____. "The book of the It." (Continued.) Archives
of Psychoanalysis 1 (1927): 670-740. Here Groddeck speaks of the unconscious as the It. The focus
is on the sadistic tendency and its relation to love
and disease.

288. _____. "Wege zum Es." (Roads to the Id.) Psychoanalyse Bewegung 4 (1932): 161-71.

289. _____. Exploring the Unconscious. New York:
Funk & Wagnalls, 1933. (Transpersonal-Spiritual
and Psycho-Personal Approaches)

290. Grof, Stanislav. Realms of the Human Unconscious.
New York: Viking Press, 1975. Grof outlines four
types of experiences which he then relates to four
realms of the unconscious. The four types of experiences include abstract or aesthetic experience,
psychodynamic experience, perinatal experience, and
transpersonal experience. He based his speculations
on the effects of LSD, which he suggests is another
"royal road" to the unconscious. (Transpersonal-
Spiritual Approach for the most part)

291. Grünbaum-Sachs, H. "Die psychologische Vorbereitung des Lehrers auf seine Aufgabe in der Erziehungsgemeinschaft in Schule und Haus. I. Tiefenpsychologie." (The psychological preparation of the teacher for his problems in the educational community in school and home. I. Psychology of the unconscious.) Pädagogisches Zentralblatt 7 (1927): 513-22. The author contends that the psychology of the unconscious (à la Freud, Adler, and Jung) is very useful to the school teacher.

292. Guitton, J. Make Your Mind Work for You. New York: Macmillan, 1958. Guitton uses a theory of the unconscious mind to account for some of the workings of the mind. (Transpersonal-Spiritual Approach)

293. Haddox, Victor. "Comparison of conscious and unconscious affect." Behavioral Science 13 (1968): 324-25. The hypothesis tested here is that the responses of a subject in a hypnotic trance are determined by his or her unconscious. The experiment involves a comparison of the effects of mood cards before and after hypnosis. No significant variance was found between the two so Haddox concluded that this experiment is evidence against the hypothesis of the repressed unconscious. (Psycho-Personal Approach)

294. Haeberlin, C. "Ueber das vital Unbewusste, Bewusstsein und Character mit Bemirkungen über die deutsche Seelenkunde von Goethe und Carus." (The vital unconscious, consciousness and character, with remarks on the German soul-study of Goethe and Carus.) Zentralblatt für Psychotherapie 8 (1935): 279-95. Haeberlin writes on the basis of an assumption of the vital psychic nature of the cosmos. (Transpersonal-Spiritual Approach)

295. Haeberlin, H. K. "The concept of the unconscious." Journal of Philosophy, Psychology and Scientific Methods 14 (1971): 544-53.

296. Hainline, R. L. "Kairos: A Jungian view of time." American Journal of Psychoanalysis 40, no. 4 (1980). Kairos is a mythical deity symbolizing the auspicious moment, eternal time, archetypal time,

when unconscious eternal time intersects our conscious, linear time. These are the moments for illumination. (Transpersonal-Spiritual Approach)

297. Haldar, R. "Art and the unconscious." Indian Journal of Psychology 10 (1935): 191-95. Art is discussed in terms of anal-eroticism, auto-eroticism, and narcissism. (Psycho-Personal Approach)

298. Hall, Marlene L. "Consciousness and the unconscious: Henry James and Jungian Psychology." Ph.D. dissertation, University of New Mexico, 1974. Hall points out the affinity between James' works and Jungian archetypal psychology. Some of the Jamesian corpus studied include Awkward Age, The Ambassadors, The Wings of the Dove, and Golden Bowl.

299. Hampden-Turner, Charles. Maps of the Mind. New York: Macmillan, 1981. This is a virtual catalog of theorists and their respective "map" of the mind. Sections relating to the topic of the unconscious are scattered throughout the book depending on whether or not a particular theorist used that term.

300. Harfst, Betsy P. "Horace Walpole and the unconscious: An experiment in Freudian analysis." Ph.D. dissertation, Northern Illinois University, 1968. Harfst maintains that works such as Castle of Otranto, Mysterious Mother, and Hieroglyphic Tales serve as wish-fulfillments for Walpole and provide us with a record of the author's own personality. (Psycho-Personal Approach)

301. Haronian, Frank. "The repression of the sublime." Synthesis 1, no. 1 (1974): 51-62. Working with the psychosynthetic model of personality (see R. Assagioli), Haronian writes about the repression of impulses and influences from the Higher Unconscious. (Transpersonal-Spiritual Approach)

302. _____. "A psychosynthetic model of personality and its implications for psychotherapy." Journal of Humanistic Psychology 15, no. 4 (Fall 1975): 25-53. Haronian considers himself a "neo-Jungian." In this article is a short description of R. Assagioli's theory of the layers of the unconscious. Also the notions intuition and inspiration are distinguished.

The latter springs from the collective unconscious,
the former from the personal unconscious.

303. Harris, Stephen Le Roy. "The mask of morality: A
study of the unconscious hypocrite in representative
novels of Jane Austen, Charles Dickens, and George
Eliot." Ph.D. dissertation, Cornell University,
1964. According to Harris the three novelists
shared a realization that morally defective but os-
tensibly respected characters (hypocrites) create
more suffering than do criminals. Here unconscious
is understood as the unawareness of oneself.
(Psycho-Personal Approach)

304. Hartmann, Eduard von. The Philosophy of the Unconscious. London: Routledge & Kegan Paul, 1950.
This is one of the landmark books on the unconscious
within the Romantic tradition. It was the book of
the nineteenth century on the subject. In this
voluminous work Hartmann attempts to show that
everything is related to and directed by The Unconscious. Hartmann, like his predecessor Carus,
distinguished three aspects of The Unconscious:
Absolute Unconscious, Physiological Unconscious,
and Psychological Unconscious. (Transpersonal-
Spiritual Approach)

305. Harvey, Robert C. "One reader reading: An exploration of the relationship between conscious and unconscious response in reading five prose fictions."
Ph.D. dissertation, University of Illinois, 1978.
The approach regarding the unconscious is psycho-
personal and founded on the ideas of psychoanalysis
as developed by Norman Holland in his book The
Dynamics of Literary Response. The five works are
taken from Tobias Smollett, Bernard Shaw, and Mrs.
Henry Wood. (Psycho-Personal Approach)

306. Haspel, K. C., and R. S. Harris. "Effects of tachistoscopic stimulation of subconscious oedipal wishes
on competitive performance: A failure to replicate."
Journal of Abnormal Psychology 91, no. 6 (Dec
1982): 437-43. (Bio-Physical and Psycho-Personal
Approaches)

307. Hayman, Anne. "What do we mean by 'Id'?" Journal
of the American Psychoanalytic Association 17

(Jan-Apr 1969): 351-80. Hayman discusses the
various theoretical problems involved in using the
construct "Id." Is it a thing or is it a logically
inferred concept? How is it to be defined or
described? She makes the point that unless there
is some consensus of meaning regarding the term
"Id" there will always be confusion surrounding the
word. What is true for the "Id" in this case is
also true for the term "unconscious." (Psycho-
Personal Approach)

308. Heaton, J. M. "Freud and Heidegger on the interpretation of slips of the tongue." Journal of the British
Society for Phenomenology 13, no. 2 (May 1982):
129-42. The differences in interpretation regarding
slips of the tongue are based on each theorists' own
understanding of the unconscious. According to
Heaton the crucial difference between Freud and
Heidegger is that they differed on what they meant
by the notion "hidden." (Psycho-Personal Approach)

309. Heilbrunn, Gert. "The neurobiologic aspect of three
psychoanalytic concepts." Comprehensive Psychiatry
2, no. 5 (1961): 261-68. Heilbrunn is attempting
to offer neurobiologic evidence to support some of
Freud's ideas. It seems, though, that Heilbrunn's
evidence for the supposed "site" of the repressed
unconscious is really evidence at best for the possible "sites" of memory. (Bio-Physical Approach)

310. _____. "Biologic correlates of psychoanalytic concepts." Journal of American Psychoanalytic Association 27, no. 3 (1979): 597-626. This is another
pro-Freudian article along the same lines as the
preceding one.

311. Heinrichs, H. Die Theorie des Unbewussten in der
Psychologie von Eduard von Hartmann. (The theory
of the unconscious in the psychology of Eduard von
Hartmann.) Bonn: Verein Studentenwehl, 1933.
(Transpersonal-Spiritual Approach)

312. Held, Fritz. "Studie zur Psychologie der Meditation
am Modell der indischen Lehren." (Study of the
psychology of meditation on the model of Indian
doctrines.) Zeitschrift für Psychotherapie und
medizinische Psychologie 5 (1955): 122-33. Held

discusses the autonomy of the spirit as having some
relationship to the psychology of the unconscious
according to psychoanalysis.

313. Hellpach, W. "Die Bewusstseins-Unbewusstseins
        Polarität der Seele." (The conscious-unconscious
        polarity of the mind.) Archiv für die gesamte
        Psychologie 96 (1936): 221-39. Hellpach reviews
        the ideas on such topics as insight, inspiration,
        foreseeing, invention, and so forth. He begins
        with the eighteenth century with the ideas of Leibnitz,
        Fichte, and others and ends with the nineteenth
        century with the ideas of Hartmann, Schelling, and
        so forth.

314. Helmholtz, H. "On perception and the unconscious
        conclusion." In A Source Book in the History of
        Psychology. Edited by R. J. Herrnstein and E. G.
        Boring. Cambridge: Harvard University Press,
        1965.

315. Herbert, S. The Unconscious in Life and Art. London:
        Allen & Unwin, 1932. The book features eight es-
        says written from a psychoanalytic point of view.
        Topics include sex, married life, self and society,
        fantasy and thought, reason and unreason, and the
        romantic spirit. McDougall and Trotter are criti-
        cized. (Psycho-Personal Approach)

316. Hermann, I. "Das Unbewusste und die Triebe vom
        Standpunkte einer Wirbeltheorie." (The unconscious
        and the instincts from the standpoint of a vortex
        theory.) Imago, Lpz. 21 (1935): 412-28.

317. Hermann, Imre. "Tudat. Tudattalan." (Consciousness
        and the unconscious.) Magyar Psychologiai Szemle
        17 (1960): 415-25. Hermann discusses the prob-
        lems and definitions of consciousness and uncon-
        scious. He also argues for a more materialistic
        interpretation of the unconscious. The importance
        of dream analysis is stressed.

318. Herron, William G. "The evidence for the uncon-
        scious." Psychoanalytic Review 49, no. 1 (1962):
        70-92. Herron asks the question whether there is
        sufficient evidence to prove that the Freudian uncon-
        scious exists. He concludes that there is. He also

distinguishes three types of unconscious: dynamic
psychological unconscious, physiological unconscious,
and physical unconscious. The third type may not
be so obvious. It refers to the totality of things
happening in the world of which a person is not
aware. The article features an extensive bibliography. (Psycho-Personal Approach)

319. Heyer, G. R. "Ein Bild aus dem unbewussten Seelenleben: die subtile Melancholie." (A picture from
the unconscious psychic life: subtle melancholy.)
Zentralblatt für Psychotherapie 7 (1934): 142-45.
Heyer is interpreting the symbolism of Dürer's en-
graving Melancholy and his Organism of the Soul.
(Psycho-Personal Approach)

320. _____. "Vom Aufbau des Unbewussten." (Reconstruction of the unconscious.) Jahrbuch für
Psychologie und Psychotherapie 1 (1953): 432-43.

321. Heyman, Steven R. "Freud and the concept of inherited
racial memories." The Psychoanalytic Review 64,
no. 3 (1977): 461-64. In this short but to-the-
point article Heyman shows that both Freud and
Jung shared similar notions of inherited racial
memories. The idea was part of the minor considerations of Freud, but for Jung it formed the
main body of his work in terms of the collective
unconscious. (Socio-Cultural Approach)

322. Hilgard, Ernest R. Unconscious Processes and Man's
Rationality. Urbana: University of Illinois Press,
1958. Clinical and laboratory evidence regarding
unconscious processes is examined. The point is
made that knowing about our own irrationality is a
triumph for rationality. (Bio-Physical and Psycho-
Personal Approaches)

323. Hill, J. C. "The unconscious mind and music."
Reiss-Davis Clinic Bulletin 12, no. 1 (Spr 1975):
30-40. Both topics are discussed from a psychoanalytic point of view. (Psycho-Personal Approach)

324. Hill, Marjorie J. "Effects of conscious and unconscious
factors on child rearing attitudes of lesbian mothers." Ph.D. dissertation, Adelphi University, 1981.
(Psycho-Personal Approach)

325. Hill, Napoleon. "The subconscious mind." In Think
     and Grow Rich. North Hollywood, Cal: Wilshire
     Book Company, 1970. Hill discusses how the sub-
     conscious can be programmed to help someone at-
     tain riches and other goals. There is very little
     theoretical discussion in the book. Hill simply
     urges us to try it and see how it works. (Trans-
     personal-Spiritual Approach)

326. Hilton, William C. "The triumph of the conservative
     unconscious in the novels of Charles Brockden
     Brown." Ph.D. dissertation, Wayne State Univer-
     sity, 1967.

327. Hinrichsen, O. ["Remarks on the creative power of
     the unconscious."] Psychiatrisch-neurologische
     Wochenschrift 41 (1939): 28-32.

328. Hochheimer, Wolfgang. "Die Rolle des Unbewussten
     im zwischenmenschlichen Verhalten." (Roles of the
     unconscious in interpersonal relations.) Psyche,
     7 (1953): 162-84 (Psycho-Personal Approach)

329. Hoffman, Cy. "Menstruation and the unconscious: A
     content analysis of dreams." Ph.D. dissertation,
     California School of Professional Psychology, 1976.
     It is argued that an archetypal principle is operating
     during menstruation and influencing collectively the
     content of dreams during this time. The theoretical
     foundation for this thesis is Jung's theory of the
     collective unconscious. Hoffman suggests that his
     study adds construct validity to Jung's ideas about
     archetypes and the collective unconscious.
     (Transpersonal-Spiritual Approach)

330. Hoffman, Russell. "The idea of the unconscious in the
     novels of Thomas Hardy." Ph.D. dissertation,
     University of California, Berkeley, 1963. Hoffman
     discusses those who influenced Hardy's understanding
     of the unconscious: Schopenhauer, Hartmann, Comte,
     Darwin, Mill, and Spencer. According to Hoffman,
     Hardy was a firm believer in the primacy and domi-
     nance of a guiding unconscious mind. (Transpersonal-
     Spiritual Approach)

331. Hook, Sidney, ed. Psychoanalysis, Scientific Method,
     and Philosophy. New York: University Press, 1959.

This is a philosophical-critical piece with various contributors discussing different aspects of the theories of psychoanalysis. (Psycho-Personal Approach)

332. Hopkins, P. "Analytic observations on the 'Scala Perfectionis' of the mystics." British Journal of Medical Psychology 18 (1939): 198-218. A psychology of the unconscious is used to interpret what Buddha, Patanjali, and others have said about the ladder to perfection. (Psycho-Personal Approach)

333. Horst, L. v. d. "Het onbewusste." (The unconscious.) Nederlandsch tijdschrift voor psychologie 4 (1937): 1-13. According to Horst, supranormal events do occur and are in part faciliated by semi-conscious or unconscious deception, but there is no need to create a separate science such as parapsychology to deal with these events. (Psycho-Personal Approach)

334. _____. "Het onderbewusste." (The subconscious.) Nederlandsch tijdschrift voor psychologie 5 (1937): 183-93. Horst outlines and discusses the content of the subconscious, which includes repressed experiences, material too weak to register in consciousness, and dispositions directly related to behavior tendencies. It is argued that instincts and intuitions operate independently of consciousness and that occult manifestations and automatisms may be explained by the subconscious.

335. _____. ["The relationship of psychology to parapsychology."] Nederlandsch Tijdschrift voor Psychologie 7 (1940): 335-46. In speculating on the possible causes of parapsychological phenomena Horst discusses the notion of "collective soul" as a possible agent involved. (Socio-Cultural and Transpersonal Spiritual Approaches)

336. Horton, R. "Destiny and the unconscious in West Africa." Africa 31 (1961): 110-16.

337. Hosiasson, S. "La suggestion et le subconscient." (Suggestion and the subconscious.) La psychologie et la vie 2 (1928): 31-35. Advice is given on how to avoid suggestions and how to make suggestions.

338. _____. "Les oublis et le subconscient." (Forgetting
      and the subconscious.) La psychologie et la vie 2
      (1928): 123-27. The author discusses various types
      of forgetting phenomena. (Psycho-Personal Ap-
      proach)

339. House, S. David. "Psychologies of the unconscious."
      Psychoanalytic Review 15 (1928): 1-26. In this
      short historical survey House reviews ideas of the
      unconscious from Plato onward. This is a good
      source for references.

340. Hubbard, La Fayette Ronald. Dianetics. Grinstead,
      England: Hubbard College of Scientology, 1967.
      In this book reference is made to the so-called
      "reactive mind" which is lodged in the subconscious
      and is the root cause of people's unhappiness.
      (Psycho-Personal and Transpersonal-Spiritual Ap-
      proaches)

341. Hubbs, Valentine C. "Consciousness and the uncon-
      scious in the dramas of Heinrich von Kleist: Kleist's
      struggle for individuation." Ph.D. dissertation,
      New York University, 1959. Hubbs maintains that
      Kleist's dramatic works were both the vehicle for
      and the products of his own struggle for psychic
      wholeness.

342. Huntley, C. W. "A study of 'unconscious' self-
      judgement." Psychological Bulletin 37 (1940): 582.
      An abstract. (Psycho-Personal Approach)

343. Ibarrola, R. "Influencia de los complejos subconscien-
      tes en la elección profesional." (The effect of sub-
      conscious complexes on vocational choice.) Psico-
      tecnia 2 (1941): 121-31. Because vocational
      choices are made not only by conscious thinking
      processes but also by unconscious factors, the au-
      thor suggests that vocational counseling should be
      equipped to investigate the subtle influences involved
      in vocational choice. Ibarrola recommends a mixed
      program using Freudian, Adlerian, and Jungian in-
      sights.

344. Ichheiser, Gustav. "On Freud's blind spots concerning
      some obvious facts." Journal of Individual Psycho-
      logy 16 (1960): 45-55. A sociopsychological model
      is proposed to replace Freud's intrapsychic one.

According to Ichheiser, Freud considered the social
dimension to be superficial. For Ichheiser the social factors are equally important in determining
what we consider reality. The point is made that
the psychology of the unconscious is not always the
answer to why a person lacks self-knowledge.
Sometimes it is a case of genuine false perception
or an error in judgment. (Psycho-Personal Approach)

345. International Encyclopedia of the Social Sciences, Vol.
1. S. v. "Analytic Psychology" by Magda Arnold.
Arnold makes a presentation of Jung's system of
ideas. Besides the presentation Arnold issues
some provocative criticisms regarding the theological implications of some of Jung's ideas. Arnold
contends that Jung's is not a Christian worldview
and that Jung's process of individuation leaves one
a veritable half-god. Both comments center on
Jung's understanding of the collective unconscious
and its relation to the person. (Transpersonal-
Spiritual Approach)

346. Jaffé, A. The Myth of Meaning. New York: Penguin
Books, Inc., 1975. Some of the sections of this
book are "The unconscious and the archetype,"
"The numinosity of the unconscious," and "The
unconscious as inner experience." The understanding of the unconscious is Jungian. (Transpersonal-
Spiritual Approach)

347. Jahn, E. "Die Bedeutung des Tiefenbewusstseins für
die religiös-ethische Erziehung." (The significance
of the unconscious for religio-ethical education.)
Pädagogisches Warte 36 (1929): 129-35. The unconscious is understood in terms of the concept of
"soul." Jahn contends that the child's soul is very
open to influences and should be instilled early with
religious and ethical motives. (Transpersonal-
Spiritual Approach)

348. Jalota, S. S. "The unconscious." Indian Journal of
Psychology 6 (1931): 157-68. For Jalota the term
"unconscious" is relatively meaningless because it
is used to account for so many different types of
experiences. He argues that it should only refer
to those latent processes which are definitely op-

posed to manifest contents of consciousness. Unconsciousness should be understood as a continuum from focal-attentive consciousness, to marginal attentive consciousness, to fore-consciousness, to primary non-conscious level, to secondary non-conscious level, to absolute non-conscious level. (Psycho-Personal Approach)

349. James, William. "Do unconscious mental states exist?" In Principles of Psychology, pp. 164-76. New York: H. Holt and Company, 1893. James presents and refutes ten alleged proofs for the existence of unconscious states. (Psycho-Personal Approach)

350. _____. The Varieties of Religious Experience. New York: Longmans, 1902. In his discussion of religious experiences James refers in places to the theory of the subconscious. At one point (p. 223) he remarks that the discovery of unconscious states is the most important step forward in psychology.

351. Janet, Pierre. "La relativité de la subconscience." (The relativity of the subconsciousness.) La psychologie et la vie 6 (1932): 3-4. It is argued that there is not any clear-cut distinction between consciousness and subconsciousness. The latter has no absolute value. See also item no. 353. (Psycho-Personal Approach)

352. Jastrow, Joseph. "On the trail of the subconscious." In The Harvey Society. The Harvey lectures 1907-1908, pp. 155-86.

353. _____. Subconscious Phenomena. Boston: R. G. Badger, 1910. The book features papers by Hugo Münsterberg, Theodore Ribot, Pierre Janet, Joseph Jastrow, Bernard Hart, and Morton Prince.

354. _____. The Subconscious. Boston and New York: Houghton, Mifflin, 1923.

355. Jelliffe, S. E. "The Parkinsonian body posture: Some considerations on unconscious hostility." Psychoanalytical Review 27 (1940): 467-79. (Psycho-Personal Approach)

356. Johnson, Paul. "Religious behavior: 1. Unconscious motivation." In Psychology and Religion, pp. 203-12.

New York: Abingdon Press, 1959. Johnson
does an excellent job of comparing and contrasting
the Freudian and Jungian ideas regarding the unconscious and its influence in religious experience.
(Psycho-Personal Approach)

357. Johnson, W. "Hegel and Freud." Monist 37 (1927):
553-77. Johnson attempts to translate Freud's
psychology of the unconscious into Hegelian terms.
(Psycho-Personal Approach)

358. Jones, Ernest. "Artistic form and the unconscious."
Mind 44 (1935): 211-15. A spokesman for psycho-
analysis writes about the creative process. (Psycho-
Personal Approach)

359. _____. "The unconscious mind and medical practice." British Medical Journal part 1 (1938): 1354-
59. Jones discusses how the unconscious of both
the doctor and the patient interferes with treatment.
(Psycho-Personal Approach)

360. Jordan, Sidney. "D. H. Lawrence's concept of the
unconscious and existential thinking." Review of
Existential Psychology and Psychiatry 5, no. 1
(1965): 34-43. See D. H. Lawrence for his understanding of the unconscious. (Transpersonal-
Spiritual Approach)

361. Joseph, Rhawn. "Awareness, the origin of thought,
and the role of conscious self-deception in resistance and repression." Psychological Reports 46
(1980): 767-81. Joseph demonstrates his agree-
ment with Sartre, Stekel, and others that what is
attributed to the agency of the unconscious can be
better understood in terms of self-deception. The
person in question does not want to know, therefore
the term "unconscious" is merely a metaphor for
this process of self-deception. (Psycho-Personal
Approach)

362. Jung, Carl Gustave. Everything Jung wrote is relevant
to the topic of the unconscious. For the sake of
economy we will simply refer to the index provided
by Carrie L. Rothgeb, editor of the Abstracts of the
Collected Works of C. G. Jung, printed by the U. S.
Government Printing Office, 1978. At the end we

will include some other sources not referred to in the Abstracts. The following entries are taken from the index of the Abstracts under the designation "unconscious." Volume numbers relate to Collected Works. (Jung's ideas regarding the unconscious cover all four approaches of the typology. For the most part, though, his ideas are weighed heavily toward the Transpersonal-Spiritual Approach and second toward the Psycho-Personal Approach.)

363. _____. "On the psychology and pathology of so-called occult phenomena: 3. Discussion of the case. The change in character. Nature of the somnabulistic attacks. Origin of the unconscious personalities." Vol. 1.

364. _____. "On the importance of the unconscious in psychopathology." Vol. 3.

365. _____. "The theory of psychoanalysis. 5. The fantasies of the unconscious." Vol. 4.

366. _____. "General description of the types. 2. The extraverted type. B. The attitude of the unconscious." Also "3. The introverted type. B. The attitude of the unconscious." Vol. 6.

367. _____. "On the psychology of the unconscious. Prefaces." Vol. 7.

368. _____. "The relations between the ego and the unconscious." Vol. 7.

369. _____. "Appendices: II. The structure of the unconscious." Vol. 7.

370. _____. "On the psychology of the unconscious." Vol. 7.

371. _____. "Instinct and the unconscious." Vol. 8.

372. _____. "On the nature of the psyche. 1. The unconscious in historical perspective. 2. The significance of the unconscious in psychology. 5. Conscious and unconscious. 6. The unconscious as a multiple consciousness." Vol. 8.

373. _____. "Archetypes of the collective unconscious." Vol. 9, part i.

374. _____. "The concept of the collective unconscious." Vol. 9, part i.

375. _____. "Conscious, unconscious, and individuation." Vol. 9, part i.

376. _____. "The role of the unconscious." Vol. 10.

377. _____. "Psychology and religion. 1. The autonomy of the unconscious." Vol. 11.

378. _____. "Foreword to White's God and the Unconscious." Vol. 11.

379. _____. "Individual dream symbolism in relation to the alchemy: A study of the unconscious processes at work in dreams." Vol. 12.

380. _____. "Religious ideas in alchemy: An historical survey of alchemical ideas. 6. Alchemical symbolism in the history of religion. I. The unconscious as the matrix of symbols." Vol. 12.

381. _____. "Paracelsus as a spiritual phenomenon. 3. The natural transformation mystery. D. The rapprochement with the unconscious." Vol. 13.

382. _____. "The philosophical tree. II. On the history and interpretation of the tree symbol. 20. The interpretation and integration of the unconscious." Vol. 13.

383. _____. "The significance of the unconscious in individual education." Vol. 17.

384. _____. "Symbols and the interpretation of dreams. 2. The functions of the unconscious." Vol. 18.

385. _____. "Two essays on analytical psychology. Foreword to the Hungarian edition of Jung: On the psychology of the unconscious." Vol. 18.

386. _____. "The archetypes and the collective unconscious." Vol. 18.

387.   . "The spirit of man, art, and literature.
           Foreword to Kankeleit: The unconscious as the
           seedbed of the creative." Vol. 18.

388.   . "Foreword." In The I Ching (Book of
           Changes.) by R. Wilhelm and C. Baynes, Prince-
           ton, N. J.: Princeton University Press, 1950.
           Jung discusses the relationship between his psycho-
           logy of the unconscious and the oriental thinking
           surrounding the I Ching.

389.   . "Consciousness and the Unconscious." In
           Psychological Reflections. (A new anthology of
           Jung's writings.) Princeton, N. J.: Princeton
           University Press, 1953.

390.   . "Confrontation with the unconscious." In
           Memories, Dreams, Reflections, pp. 170-99. New
           York: Vintage Books, 1961.

391. Jung, Carl G., and Shin-ichi Hisamatsu. "On the un-
           conscious, the self and the therapy: A dialogue."
           Psychologia: An International Journal of Psychology
           in the Orient. 11, no. 1-2 (1968): 25-32. In
           this point of interface between occidental and orien-
           tal thinking regarding the unconscious the Zen notion
           of "no mind" is related to the psychoanalytic uncon-
           scious.

392. Kamel, F. A. "The influence of the unconscious in
           parent-child relationships." Egyptian Journal of
           Psychology 6 (1951): 61-72. (Psycho-Personal
           Approach)

393. Kaplan, H.; A. Freedman; and B. Sadock, eds. "19th
           century concepts of the unconscious" and "Uncon-
           scious and bad faith." In Comprehensive Textbook
           of Psychiatry /III, Vol. 1, 3rd ed, pp. 75-76, 841-
           42. Baltimore: Williams & Wilkins, 1980. "Bad
           faith" is the expression Sartre offered to replace
           the expression "unconscious" when it came to un-
           derstanding the motivation behind certain behaviors.
           (Psycho-Personal Approach)

394.   . "The unconscious." Vol. 2, pp. 1546-47.

395. Kaplan, Martin, J. "Unconscious self evaluation and
           subliminal familiarity: An evaluation of the Wolff-

Huntley expressive behavior technique for eliciting self concepts and its relationship to subliminal familiarity. " Ph. D. dissertation, New York University, 1957. (Bio-Physical and Psycho-Personal Approaches)

396. Katan, M. "Further exploration of the schizophrenic regression to the undifferentiated state. A study of the 'assessment of the unconscious'. " International Journal of Psychoanalysis 60, part 2 (1979): 145-75. (Psycho-Personal Approach)

397. Katz, J.; J. Goldstein; and A. Dershowitz. "About 'not knowing'--Is there an unconscious?" In Psychoanalysis, Psychiatry and Law, pp. 51ff. New York: The Free Press, 1967. The authors explore the implications of a psychology of the unconscious (à la Freud) for the legal system. Also contains an account of a court hearing in New Jersey on the legality of subliminal advertisement. (Psycho-Personal Approach)

398. Keatinge, M. W. Suggestion in Education. London: Adam and Charles Black, 1911. A notion of the subconscious is used to discuss how suggestion works in education. (Psycho-Personal Approach)

399. Keehn, J. D. "Behaviorism and the unconscious. " Acta Psychologica 26 (1967): 75-78. Keehn points out that although behaviorists reject mentalistic notions such as "mind, " "conscious, " or "unconscious" they do not overlook unconscious phenomena. Regarding the latter the behaviorist prefers to interpret unconscious phenomena in terms of histories of reinforcements. In a behaviorist sense all activity is unconsciously controlled depending on the history of reinforcement. (Bio-Physical Approach)

400. Kelley, Mary B. "The unconscious rebel: Studies in feminine fiction, 1820-1880. " Ph. D. dissertation, University of Iowa, 1974. (Psycho-Personal Approach)

401. Kelloway, W. J. C. "An essay in the philosophy of mind: The Freudian unconscious. " Ph. D. dissertation, University of Ottawa, Canada, 1971. Kelloway is asking whether or not the Freudian uncon-

scious exists. In the thesis he discusses the history of the idea of the unconscious before Freud, the philosophical problems involved with the construct, the Freudian arguments for the existence of the unconscious, and the evalvation of those arguments. Kelloway contends that Freud did demonstrate the existence of the unconscious in a way that is acceptable to philosophical methods. (Psycho-Personal Approach)

402. Kelsey, Morton. God, Dreams, and Revelation. Minneapolis, Minn.: Augsbury Publishing House, 1968. Kelsey maintains that the dream, a product of the unconscious, is the means by which God communicates, indeed imparts revelations, to us. (Transpersonal-Spiritual Approach)

403. _____. Dreams: A Way to Listen to God. New York: Paulist Press, 1978. Again, in discussing dreams Kelsey refers to the unconscious as the medium through which God can and does communicate to humans. (Transpersonal-Spiritual Approach)

404. Kemper, Werner. "Analyse Zweier Eindrucksvoller Wahrtraüme." (Analysis of two striking prophetic dreams.) Psyche 8 (1954): 450-67. Kemper presents a theory regarding so-called "unconscious knowledge" that is characteristic of alleged prophetic dreams. Notwithstanding his analysis, which tends to be reductive, Kemper does not deny the possible occurrence of genuine prophetic dreams. (Psycho-Personal Approach)

405. Kennedy, J. L. "Experiments on 'unconscious' whispering." Psychological Bulletin 35 (1938): 526. An abstract.

406. Kenworthy, M. E. "The pre-natal and early post-natal phenomena of consciousness." In The Unconscious, A Symposium, pp. 178-200. Edited by C. M. Child. New York: Alfred A. Knopf, 1927. The unconscious is understood here in terms of early emotional conditioning of children via physiological influences before, during, and after birth. (Bio-Physical Approach)

407. Kiely, Bartholomew. Psychology and Moral Theology. Rome: Gregorian University Press, 1980. A

theologian explores the implications of a psychology
of the unconscious (he uses the term "subconscious")
for moral theology. He also makes reference to
what he calls the "latent self," which Kiely relates
to the "ideal self" and the "conscious actual self."
(Psycho-Personal Approach)

408. Kierkegaard, Søren. The Journals of Søren Kierkegaard, pp. 182-86. Edited by A. Dru. London:
Oxford University Press, 1938. Kierkegaard expresses his criticism of Carl Carus' ideas concerning the unconscious. Kierkegaard refers to Carus'
approach as "sophistical physiology."

409. King, C. "Religion, Psychoanalysis, Pan-Psychism."
In The Psychology of Consciousness, pp. 15-29.
London: Kegan Paul, Trench, Trübner, 1932. The
psychology of the unconscious is discussed in terms
of religious categories.

410. Klein, David B. The Unconscious--Invention or Discovery. Santa Monica, Cal.: Goodyear Publishing
Company, 1977. Klein conducts a historical-critical
inquiry regarding the construct of the unconscious.
He covers a lot of historical ground with emphasis
on Hartmann, Janet, James, Myers, Freud, and
others. Klein's agenda is to argue against any
tendency to reify the unconscious which would imply
a fragmentation of the mind. In the end he offers
an alternative understanding of what the unconscious
refers to in terms of sensory and nonsensory idea-
tion in order to perserve the one-mind paradigm.
(Psycho-Personal Approach)

411. Kleinbard, David J. "The invisible man made visible,
representation of the unconscious in the writings of
D. H. Lawrence." Ph.D. dissertation, Yale University, 1968. The author draws upon the ideas
of Freud, Laing, Piaget, Erikson, Nietzsche,
Kierkegaard, and Rilke in order to better compre-
hend how Lawrence understood the unconscious.

412. Klimo, Z. "K otazkevedomia, podvedomia, nevedomia."
(To the problem of consciousness, subconsciousness,
and nonconsciousness.) Ceskoslovenská Psychiatrie
65, no. 2 (1969): 99-103. Klimo presents the
ideas of T. Ribot regarding the question of con-

sciousness with emphasis on the physiological foundation for psychic activity. (Bio-Physical Approach)

413. Knight, Jimmie. "A description of a pedogogy for
heightening individual potential through increased
awareness of unconscious controls." Ph. D. dissertation, University of California, Los Angeles, 1980.

414. Knudsen, Harold. ["Ego-identity and the unconscious:
Further developments in psychoanalytical theory
within Günter Ammon's ego-psychology."] Dynamische Psychiatrie 9, no. 3 (1976): 163-76. According to Knudsen, Ammon designated "the unconscious"
to be that which results from or is founded on the
archaic mother-child dyad. On this foundation
creativity, ego-identity, and ego-illness depend on
the benign or maldevelopment of the childhood
symbiosis. (Psycho-Personal Approach)

415. Kockelmans, Joseph. "Daseinsanalysis and Freud's
unconscious." Review of Existential Psychology and
Psychiatry 16, no. 1 (1978-79): 21-42. Kockelmans
contends that the assumption of the unconscious is
unacceptable and superfluous. In its place he offers
the logic of daseinsanalysis as a better way to understand behavior. Ludwig Binswanger's ideas on
the topic are mentioned. (Psycho-Personal Approach)

416. Koestler, Arthur. "The unconscious before Freud."
In The Act of Creation, pp. 147-59. New York:
Dell, 1967. Koestler offers his own short version
of "the unconscious before Freud" theme. The
historical references are brief and to the point.
Also, in presenting the ideas on creativity Koestler
discusses how the unconscious is related to the act
of creation. His understanding of the unconscious
takes in account physiological, psychological, and
transpersonal factors.

417. _____. The Roots of Coincidence. New York: Vin-
tage Books, 1973. One of the theories that Koestler
presents to account for coincidences involves the
ideas of Jung and Pauli (physicist) regarding the
topic of synchronicity. For Jung the collective unconscious orchestrated coincidences. Koestler at
one point expresses his criticisms of Jung's ideas.

418. Koffka, K. "On the structure of the unconscious." In
The Unconscious, A Symposium, pp. 43-68. Edited
by C. M. Child. New York: Alfred A. Knopf,
1927. The following ideas are contrasted: 1) The
unconscious as a storehouse of static ideas according to old associationist doctrine; 2) The unconscious
as a storehouse of dynamic impulses according to
psychoanalysis; and 3) The unconscious as non-
process or physiological conditions which show certain tendencies toward completeness according to
Gestalt principles. It should be pointed out that
had Koffka entitled this article "The structure of
memory" there would not have been any loss of
meaning.

419. _____. "Unconscious." In The Principles of Ge-
stalt Psychology, pp. 51-52. New York: Harcourt,
Brace and Company, 1935. (Bio-Physical and
Psycho-Personal Approaches)

420. Kohli-Kunz, Alice. ["The so-called unconscious."]
Zeitschrift für Psychosomatische Medizin und Psychoanalyse 21, no. 3 (Jul-Sept 1975): 284-98. Regarding the phenomenon of self-deception in therapy
it is contended that Heidegger's ideas are more explanatory than Freudian theory. Freud's definition
of conscious and unconscious are critically discussed.
(Psycho-Personal Approach)

421. Kohns, Donald P. "An analysis of unconscious and
conscious professional development needs of Minnesota distributive education inservice personnel."
Ph.D. dissertation, University of Minnesota, 1975.
(Psycho-Personal Approach)

422. Kolenda, Konstantin. "Unconscious motives and human
action." Inquiry 7 (1964). An attempt is made to
discern under what circumstances it can be said that
something is done unconsciously or that unconscious
motives are at work. In one place Kolenda remarks
that repression is more akin to an illness (something that happens to a person) rather than an act of
bad will as Sartre would have argued. (Psycho-
Personal Approach)

423. Kolmerten, Carol A. "Unconscious sexual stereotyping
in utopian thought: A study of the American Owenite

communities, 1825-29." Ph.D. dissertation, Purdue
University, 1978. (Psycho-Personal Approach)

424. Korotkin, I. I., and M. M. Suslova. "Fiziologicheskoe
isledovanie neosoznanykh proiavleni i vysshei nervnoi deiatel'notti cheloveka." (Physiological study of
unconscious motivations of higher nervous activity
in man.) Zhurnal Vysshei Nervoi Deiatel'nosti 13,
no. 1 (1963): 3-10. An experiment is conducted
using both classical conditioning and hypnosis to
"confirm" Pavlov's understanding of the unconscious
as opposed to the Freudian concept. (Bio-Physical
Approach)

425. Kostandov, E. A. "Neirofiziologicheskie mekhanizmy
bessoznatel'nykh psikhicheskikh iavlenii." (Neuro-
physiologic mechanisms of unconscious phenomena.)
Uspekhi Filosofii Nauk 12, no. 4 (Oct-Dec 1981):
3-27. (Bio-Physical Approach)

426. Kranzer, Mark, ed. The Unconscious Today: Essays
in Honor of Max Schur. New York: International
Universities Press, 1971.

427. Kraus, Robert F. "Psychiatric concepts from the perspective of historical process." Pennsylvania Psychiatric Quarterly 9, no. 2 (1969): 36-40. Here
we have the psychology of the unconscious contrasted
with the ideas of E. Durkheim.

428. Krippner, Stanley. "Problems of the unconscious." In
Human Possibilities: Mind Exploration in the USSR
and Eastern Europe, pp. 194-232. Garden City,
N.Y.: Anchor Press/Doubleday, 1980. Krippner
discusses the status of the construct of the unconscious in Soviet psychology. The book contains a
good reference section. (Bio-Physical and Psycho-
Personal Approaches)

429. _____. "Access to hidden reserves of the unconscious through dreams in creative problem solving."
Journal of Creative Behavior 15, no. 1 (1981): 11-
22. Many examples of the creative dream are cited.
In one part Krippner discusses Uznadze's theory of
set as a possible explanation for the emergence at
night of answers to problems. He also speculates
about the various ways that the expression "unconscious" can be understood.

430.   Kris, E. Psychoanalytic Exploration in Art. New
        York: International Universities Press, 1952. Here
        is another case in which a psychology of the uncon-
        scious is used to interpret and understand artistic
        expression.

431.   Krisch, H. "Die Psychologie des Unbewussten von
        Carus." (Carus' psychology of the unconscious.)
        Zentralblatt für Psychotherapie 9 (1936): 283-90.
        It is argued that there is a close affinity between
        Carus' psychology of the unconscious and the under-
        standing of it by early twentieth-century depth psy-
        chologists.

432.   Kuczkowski, Richard J. "Lawrence's 'esoteric' psycho-
        logy: 'Psychoanalysis and the Unconscious' and
        'Fantasia of the Unconscious'." Ph. D. dissertation
        Columbia University, 1973. Kuczkowski presents a
        case for taking Lawrence seriously as a psychologist.
        In chapter three Lawrence's concept of the uncon-
        scious is presented in relation to William James'
        theory of emotions.

433.   Kuypers, A. Het onbewuste in de nieuwere paedago-
        gische psychologie. (The unconscious in the newer
        pedagogical psychology.) Amsterdam: H. J. Paris,
        1931. Kuypers presents a historical and theoretical
        study of the concept of the unconscious from Des-
        cartes to Freud and Adler. Adler is given special
        treatment because Kuypers thinks that Adler's ideas
        have more pedagogical significance than Freud's.
        The book has a section dealing specifically and
        practically with some aspects of a child's life.
        (Psycho-Personal Approach)

434.   Lacan, Jacques. "The Freudian unconscious and ours."
        In The Fundamental Concepts of Psycho-Analysis,
        pp. 17-28. Edited by J. Miller. New York: W.
        W. Norton and Company, 1978. Lacan also wrote
        an article in French entitled, "Unconscious, Freud,
        Language." A fuller bibliographic reference was
        not obtainable. (Psycho-Personal Approach)

435.   Lagerborg, R. "Ueber des 'unbewusste Psychisch' und
        dessen Bestimmung durch das Intentionale." (On
        the "psychological unconsciousness" and its determi-
        nation.) Forum philosophicum 1 (1930): 207-24.

Lagerborg, relying on Janet's ideas, criticizes
Ziehen, who attempted to escape the contradiction
implied by the expression "psychological unconsciousness." Lagerborg believes that the term "mind"
will completely disappear from psychology.

436. Laing, Ronald D. "The phenomena of phantasy." In
The Self and Others. Chicago: Quadrangle Books,
1962. Laing is highly critical of the psychoanalytical method of therapy. He argues that some arbitrarily attribute an unconscious when one cannot
make sense of something and arbitrarily assume no
unconscious when one can make sense of behavior.
(Psycho-Personal Approach)

437. Laird, J. "Is the conception of the unconscious of
value in psychology?" Mind 31 (1922): 433-42.
This is one third of a three-part discussion on the
topic. Laird answers "no" to the question and considers the usage of the expression "unconscious"
as a case of "trafficking in occult verbiage." He
further argues that we have no right to say that
wishes or ideas are unconscious. Laird's argument
is essentially an argument by definition. See also
F. Aveling and G. Field for the other sides of this
discussion. (Psycho-Personal Approach)

438. Lake, Frank. Clinical Theology. London: Darton
Longman & Todd, 1966. Much of Lake's work con-
firms Rank's point about the significance of the birth
experience. Lake did some of his research with
LSD as a method to retrieve early memories.
Throughout the lengthy book he makes use of the
expressions "subconscious," "unconscious" (as an
adjective), and "unconscious" (as a noun). All three
terms he defines in the glossary. Lake's understanding of the unconscious is more akin to Freud's
than to any other theorist's. Lake understood the
unconscious to be the referrent for the aggregate of
forces influencing behavior but not easily available
to consciousness. (Psycho-Personal Approach)

439. Lane, Michael. "The conscious and the unconscious in
human behavior." Science and Society 15 (1951):
303-12. This is an excellent exposition of the
Marxist psychologist alternative to psychoanalytical
terms. The author is very critical of the con-

structs of psychoanalysis. (Psycho-Personal Approach)

440. Lang, Hermann. ["The id and the unconscious: The problem of primordial structuring in psychoanaly- sis."] Revue de Psychologie et des Sciences de l'Education 10, no. 1 (1975): 71-88. (Psycho- Personal Approach)

441. Larson, Lawrence W. "Self-knowledge and the uncon- scious." Ph.D. dissertation, Stanford University, 1968. The term "unconscious" per se is discussed near the end of this study. Larson distinguishes two senses of the term. The first sense refers to one's unawareness of oneself. The second sense refers to evidence for unconscious desires and be- liefs implied in symptomatic behavior. (Psycho- Personal Approach)

442. Lasswell, H. "The changing image of human nature: Socio-cultural aspect." American Journal of Psy- choanalysis 26-27 (1966-67): 157-68. One section of this paper is entitled, "Does the unconscious undermine optimism?" Lasswell speculates on whether or not we are condemned by and to a repe- tition compulsion. He maintains that there is much evidence for an affirmative answer to the question. He makes the point that unconscious resistances to change are everpresent on the individual and the national level. He is assuming a Freudian under- standing of the construct of the unconscious. (Psycho-Personal Approach)

443. Latif, I. "The unconscious in action in industry." Indian Journal of Psychology 23 (1948): 29-30.

444. Laumonnier. "Le problêm de l'inconscient." (The problem of the unconscious.) Revue de Psychologie appliqués 36 (1927): 70-72. Laumonnier discusses what he refers to as the "true unconscious" and how it manifests itself and influences behavior.

445. Lavi, Z. "Al Tahalihim Bilti Mudaim V'Al Todaa." (Unconscious processes and consciousness.) Ofakim 7 (1953): 130-32, 142. Taking a Marxist position Lavi criticizes the Freudian system of ideas. It is argued that unconsciousness and unconscious

processes exist, but Freud underestimated the role of consciousness and the factor of social conditioning. (Psycho-Personal Approach)

446. Lawden, D. F. "On a poltergeist case." Journal of the Society for Psychical Research 50, no. 780 (June 1979): 73-76. A poltergeist event is accounted for in terms of the unconscious mind of one of the members of the "haunted" house.

447. Lawrence, D. H. Psychoanalysis and the Unconscious and Fantasia of the Unconscious. New York: Viking Press, Compass Book Edition, 1960. Lawrence understands an unconscious that is both bigger-than-life and the source of all life. There is a vitalistic biological tone to his way of writing about the unconscious. For example, he considered the great laws of the universe as the fixed habits of the "living unconscious." (Transpersonal-Spiritual Approach)

448. Lay, W. The Child's Unconscious Mind. New York: Dodd, Mead and Company, 1919.

449. Layard, J. Stone Men of Malekula. London: Chatto and Windus, 1942. The author contends that primitive ritualism is the externalization of the primordial structure and activity of the unconscious. (Socio-Cultural Approach)

450. Leak, Gary K., and Steven B. Christopher. "Freudian psychoanalysis and sociobiology, a synthesis." American Psychologist (March 1982): 313-22. The authors attempt to show that the unconscious, in the service of self-deception, makes sound evolutionary sense. Sometimes we can perform better if we fool ourselves in order to serve some selfish need. The unconscious can help us in carrying out the deception in a more effective way. This is done in the interest of survival or simply to achieve some goal. (Bio-Physical and Psycho-Personal Approaches)

451. LeBon, Gustave. The Crowd. London: Ernest Benn Limited, 1930. LeBon maintains that when people group themselves the individuality of the members tends to be lost in the crowd and somehow an agency

is created by the collectivity which then influences
the behavior of the individuals, i. e. , a "group
mind" is formed. That agency LeBon referred to
as the unconscious. (Socio-Cultural Approach)

452. _____. "La vie inconsciente et la vie collective
dans la psychologie moderne." (The subconscious
and the collective life in modern psychology.) La
Psychologie et la vie 6 (1932): 1-3. LeBon discusses two great discoveries, as he saw it, of
modern psychology; namely, the fact of subconscious
life, and the distinction between the life of an individual and the life of the group.

453. Leon, P. "Artistic form and the unconscious," Mind
44 (1935): 347-49.

454. Lepp, I. The Depth of the Soul. New York: Image
Book, 1967. (Transpersonal-Spiritual Approach)

455. Lesser, S. Fiction and the Unconscious. Boston:
Beacon Press, 1957. (Psycho-Personal Approach)

456. Leuner, H. "Guided affective imagery: An account
of its development." Journal of Mental Imagery 1
(1977): 73-92. Leuner accepts Freud's basic assumption that unconscious motivations influence behavior, even the nature of the contents of imagina-
tive experiences. Leuner's point is that imaginal
behavior, facilitated by the technique of guided affective imagery, will give the therapist insight into
the patient's unconscious behavioral tendencies and
adaptive attitudes. In short, Leuner offers another
"royal road" to the unconscious. (Psycho-Personal
Approach)

457. Levin, David M. "Picturing the Freudian Unconscious."
Psychoanalytic Review 68, no. 2 (Sum 1981): 255-
63. Levin finds Freud's topographical model of the
psyche inadequate. Levin offers a "unified field
theory" as an alternative explanation regarding behavior usually explained in terms of the unconscious.
He also draws a fine line between what can be considered "accidental" and "deliberate." (Psycho-
Personal Approach)

458. Levine, Conalee. "A comparison of the conscious and
unconscious identifications with both parental figures

among addicted and non-addicted male adolescent character disorders." Ph.D. dissertation, New York University, 1959. In this experimental study involving 20 addicts and 20 non-addicts Levine found that, for the most part, both groups showed similar patterns. (Psycho-Personal Approach)

459. Levine, Israel. The Unconscious; An Introduction to Freudian Psychology. New York: Macmillan, 1923. Besides being an introduction this book discusses the question of validity regarding the unconscious, the significance of the unconscious for education, crowd psychology, personality, ethics, aesthetics, and philosophy. (Psycho-Personal Approach)

460. Levine, Jacques. ["The unconscious at school."] Etudes Psychotherapiques no. 23 (Mar 1976): 3-65. The ideas of eleven authors are presented regarding the question of how pupils and teachers are influenced by unconscious processes.

461. Levy, Donald. "Philosophical criticisms of the unconscious in psychoanalysis." Ph.D. dissertation, Cornell University, 1980. Levy presents and attempts to refute the arguments of Wittgenstein, James, and MacIntyre against the scientific status of the construct of the unconscious. Levy finds their arguments weak. He admits, though, that he did not prove that psychoanalysis is a science. (Psycho-Personal Approach)

462. Lewes, G. H. "The general mind." In Problems of Life and Mind, pp. 159-70. Boston: Houghton, Osgood and Company, 1879. (Socio-Cultural Approach)

463. Lewis, Clifford L. "John Steinbeck: Architect of the Unconscious." Ph.D. dissertation, University of Texas at Austin, 1972. According to Lewis, Steinbeck was a great expounder of the importance of the unconscious as an influencer in one's life. He sought the explanation for group behavior in the archaic experiences of a "common unconscious." (Socio-Cultural Approach)

464. Lewis, Geneviève. Le problèm de l'inconscient et le cartésianism. (The problem of the unconscious and

Cartesianism.) Paris: Presses Universitaires de France, 1950. Besides the topic of consciousness and unconscious Lewis also discusses the notion of soul according to Cartesian theologians.

465. Lewis, I. "The anthropologist's encounter with the supernatural." Parapsychology Review 5, no. 2 (1974): 5-9. It is argued that many supernatural experiences reveal more about the subconscious needs of the person than about the supernatural. Even so, according to Lewis, we cannot catagorically deny that spiritual forces exist outside the agency of a person's subconscious. (Psycho-Personal Approach)

466. Lilly, J. C. The Center of the Cyclone (An autobiography of inner space). New York: Julian Press, 1972. With the help of LSD Lilly attempts to chart the map of the various levels of consciousness. Although he did not explicitly devote a section to the topic of the unconscious, it is not difficult to see that some of the states of consciousness that he described would have been found descriptive of the unconscious by others. For example, R. Assagioli's construct of the Higher Unconscious seems to correspond to some of the states that Lilly describes. There are also parallels to the psychic maps of Stanislav Grof and Kenneth Ring.

467. Linford, James L. "Conscious and unconscious moral judgement, moral character and conventional conduct in adolescence." Ph.D. dissertation, California School of Professional Psychology, 1977. This experimental study involves a group of seventeen-year-old male, Catholic high school seniors. (Psycho-Personal Approach)

468. Lipps, Theodor. "Der Begriff des Unbewussten in der Psychologie." Records of the Third International Congress of Psychology, Munich. (1897). Freud cites this reference in his Interpretation of Dreams (p. 611).

469. Littner, Ner. "Usefulness of psychoanalytic theory, discussion." Smith College Studies in Social Work 37, no. 2 (1967): 119-26. According to Littner the theory of the unconscious is useful because con-

scious aspects of a person's communication do not
tell the whole story about the person. Even so,
we do not want to imply that a person has two
minds requiring two different professions for understanding. Also Littner contends that resistance to
the concept of the unconscious is really a refusal
to accept certain knowledge of oneself. (Psycho-
Personal Approach)

470. Long, Constance. Psychology of Phantasy. London:
      Baillière, Tindall and Cox, 1920. Much of the
      book is devoted to the psychology of the unconscious
      and children. She discusses unconscious factors in
      sex education, unconscious symbolism in dreams,
      evidence of the unconscious mind in children, and
      other subjects. She also reviews Jung's "The Psy-
      chology of the Unconscious." (Psycho-Personal and
      Transpersonal-Spiritual Approaches)

471. Long, Lewis M. "Alfred Adler and the problem of the
      unconscious." American Journal of Individual Psy-
      chology 11 (1954-55): 163-66. Adler understands
      the expression "unconscious" to refer to the mis-
      understood aspects of one's life-style and not as
      something that has a separate, distinct existence in
      the psyche. (Psycho-Personal Approach)

472. Lotto, David J. "Another point of view on Freud's
      metapsychology," Journal of the American Academy
      of Psychoanalysis 10, no. 3 (Jul 1982): 457-81.
      Lotto argues in favor of Freud's metapsychology.
      Fifty-four references are cited. (Psycho-Personal
      Approach)

473. Lowe, Walter James. "Mystery and the unconscious:
      A study in the thought of Paul Ricoeur." Ph.D.
      dissertation, Yale University, 1972. The notion of
      "mystery" is derived from Gabriel Marcel. Two
      works by Paul Ricoeur are discussed: L'homme
      faillible and De l'interpretation. The latter work
      centers on the Freudian understanding of the uncon-
      scious. Lowe offers his study as a point of inter-
      face between theology and psychoanalysis. (Psycho-
      Personal Approach)

474. _____. Evil and the Unconscious. New York: Scho-
      lars Press, 1983. The book centers on how psy-

choanalysis addresses the problem of evil and suffering. (Psycho-Personal Approach)

475. Loye, David. "The pooling of vision." In The Know-
able Future, pp. 123-49. New York: Wiley, 1978.
Loye discusses how the unconscious can facilitate
predictions about the future. He even ties the research into the topic of the unconscious to the U.S.-
USSR power struggle. He suggests that the U.S.
Department of Defense should be very interested in
the topic of the unconscious. (Transpersonal-
Spiritual Approach)

476. Lubac, E. Les niveaux de conscience et d'inconscience
et leurs intercommunications. (The levels of consciousness and unconsciousness and their intercommunications.) Paris: Alean, 1929. Lubac calls
unconscious that form of psychological life which
pursues its course at one or at several levels
totally distinct from that of consciousness. He attempts to determine these levels. Part of the book
is devoted to discussions regarding dream consciousness.

477. Lucas, F. L. Literature and Psychology. London:
Carsell, 1951. The book features the ideas of
Freud and Stekel regarding the interpretation and
judgment of literature. Two different psychologies
of the unconscious are brought to bear on the topic.
(Psycho-Personal Approach)

478. Lynch, D. "Creative flashes from the Twilight Zone."
Science Digest (Dec 1981): 69-71, 94. The cover
title reads "Creative fire: Summon it from your
unconscious mind." (Transpersonal-Spiritual
Approach)

479. Machotka, Otakar. The Unconscious in Social Relations.
New York: Philosophical Library, 1964. The book
should have been entitled, "Unconscious Processes
in Social Relations." Indeed, Machotka catalogues
the thousand and one subtle processes that go on
in social environments. He describes the many un-
noticed ways we learn, communicate, understand one
another, respond, and perform certain activities
without deliberate, direct attention to what we are
doing. A very thorough book on the topic. Despite

the noun form usage of the term "unconscious" in
the title, Machotka hardly ever uses the term in
that form again. He uses it almost exclusively in
its adjectival form, hence the suggestion that the
title is misleading and should have been worded
differently. (Psycho-Personal Approach)

480. MacIntyre, Alasdair C. The Unconscious. London:
Routledge & Kegan Paul, 1958. MacIntyre applies
his philosophical-critical expertise to discuss the
Freudian unconscious. MacIntyre accepts the reality of unconscious processes but not the reality of
"the unconscious" in any reified sense. He argues
that Freud's hypothesis of the unconscious is a
legitimate assumption but not as an explanatory
concept. It is a descriptive concept. Besides
critiquing Freud, MacIntyre gives a good accounting of how the construct of the unconscious functions
within the Freudian system of ideas. (Psycho-
Personal Approach)

481. Mahony, P. "Archeologist in psychiatry." Contemporary Psychoanalysis 10, no. 1 (1974): 143-53.
Mahony reviews Henri Ellenberger's The Discovery
of the Unconscious. See also H. Ellenberger.

482. Mandolini, I. "La simulacion inconsciento." (Unconscious simulation.) Archivo argentinos psicologie
norm patol 1 (1933): 17-18. The author wrote
within the psychoanalytic framework.

483. Mare, W. de la. Behold, this dreamer! Of reverie,
night, sleep, dream, love-dreams, nightmare,
death, the unconscious, the imagination, divination,
the artist, and kindred subjects. New York:
Knopf, 1939.

484. Margetts, Edward L. "The concept of the unconscious
in the history of medical psychology." Psychiatric
Quarterly 27 (1953): 115-38. This is a good,
short history on the topic with many references.
Margetts cites the names and ideas of many who
after 1850 indicated in their writings that they were
familiar with the existence of mental activity outside of our waking consciousness.

485. Marshall, James. Intention in Law and Society. New
York: Funk & Wagnalls, 1968. Among the topics

he discusses, Marshall devotes a section to how the
unconscious and the question of intention relate to
the legal process. (Psycho-Personal Approach)

486.   Martin, Alexander R.   "Karen Horney's theory in
       today's world." American Journal of Psychoanaly-
       sis 35, no. 4 (Win 1975): 297-302.   Among other
       topics Martin discusses Horney's ideas about uncon-
       scious healing forces. (Psycho-Personal Approach)

486a. Martin, Joseph.   The Power of Your Subconscious
       Mind.   Toronto and New York: Bantam Books,
       1982.   (Transpersonal-Spiritual Approach)

487.   Martin, Michael.   "The explanatory value of the uncon-
       scious."   Philosophy of Science 31, no. 2 (1964):
       122-32.   Martin contends that A. Pap and A. Mac-
       Intyre have invalid arguments against the Freudian
       theory of the unconscious as being considered an
       explanatory theory. (Psycho-Personal Approach)

488.   Martin, P. W.   Experiment in Depth.   New York:
       Pantheon, 1955.   Martin is essentially working
       within a Jungian frame of reference when he writes
       about the "inner world." He discusses such things
       as ego, persona, anima, animus, Self, dreams,
       phantasy, visions, and the individuation process.
       He also draws on the ideas of Eliot and Toynbee.
       (Transpersonal-Spiritual Approach)

489.   Masek, Robert J.   "The problem of approach in a psy-
       chology of the unconscious." Ph.D. dissertation,
       University of Regina, Canada, 1981.   The thesis
       centers around the Freudian understanding of the
       unconscious. Masek argues that the approach of
       psychoanalysis is a dated natural science approach
       which leads to empirical difficulties in how human
       phenomena are viewed. His alternative is based on
       a phenomenological approach which can avoid some
       of the difficulties. (Psycho-Personal Approach)

490.   Maslow, Abraham.   "The changing image of human
       nature: The psychological aspect." American
       Journal of Psychoanalysis 26-27 (1966-67): 148-57.
       One of the points he makes is that understanding
       the unconscious determinants of behavior and moti-
       vation fosters humility and clearer insight into one-

self and the universe. We could also mention that
Maslow, in his book Toward a Psychology of Being
(p. 171), refers to the unconscious as the source
of health and creativity. It is not, as some believe,
merely the source of negative forces.

491. Maslow, Paul. The Individual Through the Rorschach.
Volume 1 of The Life Science. Brooklyn, N.Y.:
Author, 1951. The Roschach test and technique is
offered as another "road" to the unconscious.
(Psycho-Personal Approach)

492. _____. Powers of the Mind, Volume II of The Life
Science. Brooklyn, N.Y.: Author, 1952. Maslow
discusses such topics as inner personality, mysticism, genetic forgetting, moral consciousness,
faith and doubt, and so forth.

493. Matte-Blanco, Ignacio. "Expression in symbolic logic
of the charactersistics of the system unconscious."
International Journal of Psycho-Analysis 40, part 1
(1959): 1-5. Matte-Blanco translates some of
Freud's findings into logico-mathematical terms.
(Psycho-Personal Approach)

494. _____. The Unconscious as Infinite Set. New York:
Duckworth, 1975. This is the massive version of
the author's program to translate Freudian psychology into symbolic logic that was outlined in the
previous article.

495. Mauco, G. "La psychologie de l'enfant dans ses rapports avec la psychologie de l'inconscient." (The
relationships between child psychology and the psychology of the unconscious.) Revue française de
psychanalyse 9, no. 4 (1936): 430, 658. (Psycho-
Personal Approach)

496. _____. La psychologie de l'enfant dans ses rapports
avec la psychologie de l'inconscient. (Child psychology in relation to the psychology of the unconscious.) Paris: Denoël & Steele, 1938. The
author discusses some of the similarities between
the unconscious and childish thinking, such as
identification, precausality, synchronism, non-
contradiction, juxaposition, symbolism, and animism.
Mauco also compares the ideas of Piaget and Freud
on the topic.

497. May, Rollo. "Creativity and the unconscious." Humanitas 1, no. 3 (1966): 295-311. May contends that the unconscious does not exist as such, but the expression "the unconscious" is shorthand standing for the potentialities for awareness, experience and action which the individual up to that moment cannot or will not actualize. (Psycho-Personal Approach)

498. McDougall, William. The Group Mind. New York: G. P. Putnam's Sons, 1920. (Socio-Cultural Approach)

499. Meadel, G. ["Unconscious suicides."] Perspectives Psychiatriques 3, no. 47 (1974): 173-81. Meadel contends that some so-called accidental deaths are really cases of unconscious suicides. A case in point is presented and discussed. (Psycho-Personal Approach)

500. Meissner, W. W. "Affective response to psychoanalytic death symbols." Journal of Abnormal Social Psychology 56 (1958): 295-99. This is an experimental study in support of the psychoanalytic theory of unconscious affective reactions regarding death symbols. (Psycho-Personal Approach)

501. Menard, P. L'écriture et le subconscient: psychanalyse et graphologie. (Handwriting and the subconscious: psychoanalysis and graphology.) Paris: Alcan, 1931. Menard maintains that handwriting analysis is a road to the unconscious. According to Menard this type of analysis can reveal the inferior but not the superior psychism. (Psycho-Personal Approach)

502. Mendel, Werner M. "My dreams as psychotherapy supervisor." Voices 3, no. 2 (1967): 36-41. Mendel uses dreams as a compass to determine the direction therapy should take. Sometimes the direction in question is not obvious but subtle. In other words, the unconscious knows better. (Psycho-Personal Approach)

503. Mendelsohn, E., and L. H. Silverman. "Effects of stimulating psychodynamically relevant unconscious fantasies on schizophrenic psychopathology." Schizophrenia Bulletin 8, no. 3 (1982): 532-47. See also L. Silverman. (Psycho-Personal Approach)

504. Menninger, William C. "The theory of the unconscious."
Journal of the Kansas Medical Society 44-45 (1943-
44): 183-86. Menninger's thoughts are orientated
toward the Freudian understanding of the unconscious.
He discusses eight areas that have been cited as
evidence for the unconscious, such as dreams, slips,
hypnotic phenomena, forgetting, unexplained solutions
of problems, psychotic speech, small amount of
conscious material, and forgotten childhood experiences. He also outlines seven characteristics of
the unconscious: dynamic, infantile, regressive,
timelessness, illogical, nonverbal, and working on
a pleasure-pain principle. (Psycho-Personal
Approach)

505. Merlin, Eugene. "Jung and TA: Some clarifications."
Transactional Analysis Journal 6, no. 2 (Apr 1976):
169-72. Here we have the constructs of the personal and collective unconscious compared and contrasted between the Jungian and Transactional
Analysis frameworks.

506. Metzner, R. "Ten classical metaphors of self-trans-
formation." Journal of Transpersonal Psychology
12, no. 1 (1980): 47-62. In one place Metzner
refers to the collective unconscious as the storehouse of the accumulated wisdom of the human
race. He refers to the "Higher Self" which can
awaken sleeping memories as well as send us messages from the future. (Transpersonal-Spiritual
Approach)

507. Meyer, Adolf E. "Probleme der Es-Ich-Überlich
Gliederung." (Problems of the id-ego-superego
articulation.) Psyche 23, no. 8 (1969): 561-91.
Meyer critically evaluates the relationship between
the terms id-ego-superego and the constructs conscious-unconscious. He concludes that the uncon-
scious-preconscious discussion is obsolete. He
maintains that the cybernetic model of Waelder is
useful in understanding the boundary relationship
between the id and the ego.

508. Midwest Research, Inc. 6515 Highland Road, Suite
203-1121, Pontiac, Michigan 48054. This company
sells subliminal audiotapes that are supposed to
activate the subconscious mind in order to do such
things as develop one's psychic power, increase

self-confidence, expand creativity, increase sexual pleasure, improve athletic skills, motivate for success, and other things. (Transpersonal-Spiritual Approach)

509. Milan, Mikulas. ["The role of the unconscious in child performance."] Psychologia a Patopsychologia Dietata 9, no. 3 (1974): 241-46. The author discusses the role of unconscious motives and unconscious attitudes in various learning tasks of children. (Psycho-Personal Approach)

510. _____. ["The set and process of learning."] Jednotna Skola 26, no. 6 (Jun 1974): 539-53. Milan features the Georgean School of psychology, which was founded by N. Uznadze in 1921. Among the topics presented are unconscious psychical processes, subconscious mind, and the possibility of better controlling behavior through the knowledge of the unconscious. (Bio-Physical and Psycho-Personal Approaches)

511. Miller, I. "Unconscious fantasy and masturbatory technique." Journal of the American Psychoanalytic Association 17 (1969): ?-849. It is contended that the masturbatory technique itself can be interpreted as manifest content facilitating some unconscious fantasy. (Psycho-Personal Approach)

512. Miller, James G. Unconsciousness. New York: John Wiley & Sons, 1942. This is a most thorough book on the topic of the unconscious especially in relation to the laboratory and clinical uses of the term. In trying to clarify some of the language surrounding the topic of the unconscious Miller outlines, discusses, and illustrates sixteen definitions of what "unconscious" can refer to. The sixteen include the following list of descriptive categories: Inanimate, absent-minded, not-mental, undiscriminating, conditional, unsensing, unattending, lacking insight, unremembering, acting involuntarily, acting instinctively, unrecognizing, unable to communicate, ignoring, not in consciousness, and unaware of discrimination. Miller suggests that we use these expressions in scientific writing and avoid the vague term "unconscious." Miller also distinguishes the following types of unconsciousness: subliminal un-

consciousness, inattentive unconsciousness, insightless unconsciousness, forgetful unconsciousness,
inherited unconsciousness, involuntary unconsciousness, and incommunicable unconsciousness. (Bio-
Physical and Psycho-Personal Approaches)

513. _____. "The experimental study of unconscious
processes." In Feelings, and Emotions: The
Mooseheart Symposium, pp. 261-67. Edited by
M. L. Reymert. New York: McGraw-Hill, 1950.
Miller argues that there are many levels of unconsciousness. The distinctions of merely conscious
and unconscious is too simple.

514. _____. "Unconscious processes and perception."
In Perception: An Approach to Personality. Edited
by R. R. Blake and G. V. Ramsey. New York:
Ronald Press Company, 1951. Miller makes the
point that the primary principle behind our perceptual processes, conscious and unconscious, is not
rationality but the process of irrational belief.
Seventy references are cited.

515. Miller, Milton L. "An unconscious attitude toward the
stock market." Psychiatric Forum 5, no. 1 (Win
1975): 1-3. This is a case study of a man's unconscious urge to lose money and its relationship
to his father-figure. (Psycho-Personal Approach)

516. Miller, S. "Dialogue with the Higher Self." Synthesis
1, no. 2 (1975): 122-39. Miller is working with
R. Assagioli's model of the psyche which includes
the Lower, Middle, and Higher Unconscious. In
this piece Miller is giving advise on how to contact
the Higher Self for answers. (Transpersonal-
Spiritual Approach)

517. Mindell, Arnold P. "Synchronicity: An investigation
of the unitary background patterning synchronous
phenomena. (A psychoid approach to the unconscious.)." Ph.D. dissertation, Union Graduate
School, Midwest, 1972. Mindell presents a holistic
method of comprehending parapsychological or synchronistic events. Specifically he discusses in de-
tail meaningful coincidences involving death, love,
psychosis, and so forth. Also an attempt is made
to relate psychic patterns and physical laws. For

the most part Mindell's method is based on the
practice of amplification and the investigation of
archetypal motifs. (Transpersonal-Spiritual
Approach)

518.   Mintz, Ira. "The anniversary reaction: A response
        to the unconscious sense of time." Journal of the
        American Psychoanalytic Association 19 (1971):
        720-35. Working within a Freudian framework
        Mintz makes the point that the unconscious remem-
        bers and that conscious or unconscious stimuli can
        reactivate the painful experiences. (Psycho-Personal
        Approach)

519.   Mitchell, E. D. "Outer space to inner space: An
        astronaut's odyssey." Saturday Review (Feb 1975):
        20-21. Although not explicitly on the unconscious
        Mitchell discusses the need for "psychonauts" to
        make the "inner journey." He argues that we need
        more input from intuitive-subjective modes of con-
        sciousness as opposed to rational-objective-material-
        ist modes. He implies that such input is necess-
        ary for planetary survival.

520.   Modjeska, C. N. "A note on unconscious structure in
        the anthropology of Edward Sapir." American An-
        thropologist 70, no. 2 (1968): 344-48. Modjeska
        discusses the controversy between Boss and Sapir
        over language structure and how their respective
        understanding of the unconscious is involved.
        (Psycho-Personal Approach)

521.   Money-Kyrle, R. E. Psychoanalysis and politics: A
        contribution to the psychology of politics and morals.
        New York: W. W. Norton, 1951. The author in-
        vestigates the unconscious processes, fantasies,
        and motives that play a part in the political life of
        the individual and groups. (Psycho-Personal and
        Socio-Cultural Approaches)

522.   _____. "The world of the unconscious and the world
        of commonsense." British Journal for the Philoso-
        phy of Science 7 (1956): 86-96. According to the
        author the world of the unconscious has its beginning
        in the first few months of life and survives in the
        unconscious. It is not long after that the world of
        common sense develops with the rise of ego centri-

city and dualistic categories. (Psycho-Personal Approach)

523. Montmasson, J. M. Le rôle de l'inconscient dans l'invention scientifique. (The role of the unconscious in scientific invention.) Paris: Alcan, 1928. In this book Montmasson refers to the automatic unconscious, the dynamic unconscious, and the esthetic unconscious. All three play a part in the process of invention, be it in the area of mathematics, natural or moral sciences. The book features one hundred and fifty items in the bibliography. (Bio-Physical, Psycho-Personal, and Transpersonal-Spiritual Approaches)

524. _____. Invention and the Unconscious. New York: Harcourt, Brace, 1932. According to Montmasson the unconscious is found as the mysterious agent of mental transformation in all phases of knowledge. He discusses three aspects of the unconscious: the automatic, the dynamic, and the esthetic.

525. _____. "Discipliner le subconscient pour inventor." (The discipline of the subconscious for the purposes of invention.) La Psychologie et la vie 6 (1932): 22-24. He makes the curious statement that our subconsciousness is a psychological activity which is more or less conscious in itself. Montmasson suggests that we discipline the subconscious in order for it to function better in the process of invention.

526. Moore, J. S., and K. Dunlap. "Discussion: consciousness, the unconscious, and mysticism." Philosophical Review 37 (1928): 72-74. The discussion involves the distinctions between real and pseudomysticism, and the different meanings of the unconscious.

527. Moore, M. S. "Responsibility for unconsciously motivated action." International Journal of Law Psychiatry 2, no. 3 (1979): 323-47. The article is based on a Freudian understanding of the unconscious. (Psycho-Personal Approach)

528. Moore, Thomas V. The Driving Forces of Human Nature. New York: Grune and Stratton, 1948. Moore refers to the unconscious as the unconscious

personality, a hibernating beast that is ever active and in need of a system of control. In another place he calls the subconscious personality the sum total of the contrary trends of the well organized personality. The term "personality" is used in the empirical sense and not in the metaphysical sense. (Psycho-Personal Approach)

529. Morales, Armando. "The collective preconscious and racism." Social Casework 52, no. 5 (1971): 285-93. Morales conducts an interesting discussion on the relationship between the construct of the collective preconscious (as opposed to collective unconscious) and racism. This is a good example of how a theoretical change in a concept can have serious socio-political overtones. (Socio-Cultural Approach)

530. Moreno, Mario. "Collective conscious and collective unconscious in the genesis of neurosis." Psychotherapy and Psychosomatics 15, no. 1 (1967): 48. An abstract. Moreno contends that the collective conscious is equally important as the collective unconscious. He feels that Jungians have overstressed the latter at the expense of the former. (Socio-Cultural Approach)

531. Mowrer, O. Hobart. "Changing conceptions of the unconscious." Journal of Nervous and Mental Disease 129 (1959): 222-34. Mowrer's ideas on the topic of the unconscious are best understood if one keeps in mind that for Mowrer the unconscious and conscience were synonymous. This is true for this article and the succeeding references. (Transpersonal-Spiritual Approach)

532. _____. "The unconscious re-examined in a religious context." In Psychology and Religion. Edited by O. Strunk. New York: Abingdon Press, 1959.

533. _____. "Communication, conscience, and the unconscious." Journal of Communication Disorders 1 (1967): 109-35.

534. Mullane, Harvey. "Discussion: Unconscious and disguised emotions." Philosophy and Phenomenological Research 36, no. 3 (Mar 1976): 403-11. Mullane

replies to criticism by Michael Fox of the
Mullane analysis of unconscious emotional states.
Mullane contends that there can be unconscious
emotional states by distinguishing disposition and
experience. One can be afraid even though one does
not feel afraid. (Psycho-Personal Approach)

535. Müller-Hegemann, D. "Bemerkkungen zur Narkoana-
lyse." (Remarks on narcoanalysis.) Psychiatrie,
Neurologie und medizinische Psychologie 6 (1954):
3-8. The author is arguing for the primacy of consciousness and against the claim that narcoanalysis
is dealing with unconscious material. (Psycho-
Personal Approach)

536. Murphy, J. The Power of Your Subconscious Mind.
Englewood Cliffs, N. J.: Prentice-Hall, 1963.
(Transpersonal-Spiritual Approach)

537. Murray, Gilbert. "Inherited Conglomerate." In Greek
Studies, pp. 66f. Oxford: Clarendon Press, 1946.
Although Murray did not use the expression "unconscious," the inherited conglomerate can be considered an implicit example of the unconscious according to the Socio-Cultural Approach.

538. Myers, Frederick W. H. Science and a Future Life.
London: Macmillan, 1893. Myers is known for
the expression "subliminal self." He also used
the expressions "unconscious self" and "transcen-
dental self." Essentially the expressions can be
considered synonymous. In this book Myers is
making a case for life after death. (Transpersonal-
Spiritual Approach)

539. _____. Human Personality and Its Survival of
Bodily Death. New York: Longmans, Green, and
Company, 1907.

540. Myerson, Paul G. "Assimilation of unconscious material." International Journal of Psycho-Analysis
44, no. 3 (1963): 315-27. (Psycho-Personal
Approach)

541. Nameche, Gene F. "Two pictures of man." Journal
of Humanistic Psychology 1, no. 1 (1966): 70-88.
Rogerian and Freudian "pictures" of humankind

are presented. Here we have the Rogerian understanding of what "unconscious" refers to compared
to Freud's. (Psycho-Personal Approach)

542. Nash, Laura J. "Relation between sexual object choice
of women and ego development, neuroticism, and
conscious and unconscious sexual identity." Ph. D.
dissertation, Hofstra University, 1976. (Psycho-
Personal Approach)

543. Nastovic, Ivan. [The hypothesis of the familial unconscious.] Anali Zavoda za Mentalno Zdravlje 5, no.
4 (1973): 85-104. Nastovic presents the ideas of
L. Szondi regarding the familial unconscious and
relates them to the theories of Freud and Jung.

544. Navradszky, Laszlo I. "Mechanism of defense: A
tachistoscopic demonstration of perceptual defense
against a hypnotically intensified unconscious conflict." Ph. D. dissertation, Brigham Young University, 1980. (Bio-Physical and Psycho-Personal
Approaches)

545. Netherton, Morris, and N. Shiffrin. Past Lives Therapy. New York: William Morrow, 1978. Patients
are helped with current problems by working through
prenatal, natal, or previous lives events. It is
maintained that the unconscious mind facilitates such
a process. (Psycho-Personal and Transpersonal-
Spiritual Approaches)

546. Neuman, J. "The existence of the Freudian unconscious in the structure and function of the nervous
system." Psychoanalytic Review 36 (1949): 355-64.
This article involves a curious blend of Freudian
terminology and neurophysiology in the attempt to
find the physical site of the unconscious. Neuman
maintains that the cerebral cortex contains two
distinct tissues; namely, one in the service of ontogenetic experience, and the other in the service of
phylogenetic experiences. (Bio-Physical Approach)

547. Neumann, Erich. Art and the Creative Unconscious.
Princeton, N. J.: Princeton University Press, 1959.
(Transpersonal-Spiritual Approach)

548. _____. Depth Psychology and a New Ethics. London: Hodder & Stoughton, 1969. Neumann attempts

to draw ethical conclusion from a psychology of the unconscious according to the Jungian school of thought.

549. Neumann, J. "Das Unbewusste in der Verkündigung Johannes Müllers." (The unconscious in the writings of Johannes Müller.) Zeitschrift für Religious psychologie 3 (1930): 37-46.

550. Newman, Ernest. The Unconscious Beethoven, An Essay in Musical Psychology. New York: Knopf, 1930.

551. Nikelly, Arthur. "The Adlerian concept of the unconscious in psychotherapy." Journal of Individual Psychology 22 (1966): 214-21. According to Nikelly, Adler did not understand the conscious-unconscious relationship as one involving two distinct and separable categories but more along the lines of a continuum. Nikelly also pointed out that sometimes a patient can use the construct of the unconscious as an excuse for avoiding personal responsibility. (Psycho-Personal Approach)

552. Nimier, J. "Role de l'inconscient dans l'attitude des eleves a l'egard des mathematiques." (The role of the unconscious in the attitude of students toward mathematics.) Psychiatrie de l'Enfant 23, no. 2 (1980): 383-460. (Psycho-Personal Approach)

553. Nolan, Paul. "Saint Thomas and the Unconscious mind." Ph.D. dissertation, The Catholic University of America, 1954. Aquinas never used the expression "unconscious mind," but Nolan's work is another good source for investigating the idea of the unconscious before the word itself was coined.

554. Northridge, W. L. Modern Theories of the Unconscious. London: Kegan Paul, Trench, Trübner & Company, 1924. (Psycho-Personal Approach)

555. Noval, Martin. "The unconscious in Freud and Breton." Ph.D. dissertation, University of Waterloo, Canada, 1973. This study centers on the notions of the "marvelous" and the "uncanny" and how Freud and the surrealist poet André Breton understood events characterized by those two words.

556. Odajnyk, V. W. "Politics and the unconscious." In
     Jung and Politics, pp. 67-85. New York: Harper
     & Row, 1976. Odajnyk attempts to interpret certain
     political behaviors in terms of a psychology of the
     unconscious according to Jung. This section centers
     on the topics "shadow" and projection. (Socio-
     Cultural Approach)

557. Osler, Geoffrey F. "The changing image of human
     nature: The biological aspect." American Journal
     of Psychoanalysis 26-27 (1966-67): 130-38. Osler
     makes reference to such things as a Biologic Brain
     which could be the physical base for the Id, and
     that the species-specific stimulus-bound patternings
     of the Biologic Brain could be related to Jung's
     "Universal Unconscious." (Bio-Physical Approach)

558. Packard, Vance. "So ad men become depth men."
     In The Hidden Persuaders. New York: Pocket
     Books, 1980. This section discusses subliminal
     advertising. The author is working with a model
     of the mind that includes three levels--conscious,
     subconscious, and a third level, which is unnamed
     but could be considered the repressed unconscious.
     Many references are cited relative to subliminal
     advertisement.

559. Palmer, J., and J. Altrocchi. "Attribution of hostile
     intent as unconscious." Journal of Personality 35,
     no. 1 (1967): 164-76. This is an experimental
     study. (Psycho-Personal Approach)

560. Papageorgis, Demetrios. "Repression and the uncon-
     scious: A social psychological reformulation."
     Journal of Individual Psychology 21, no. 1 (1965):
     18-31. This is a landmark piece of literature be-
     cause the author assembles and makes reference
     to most of the relevant sources on the topic. He
     offers eight alternative ways to interpret behavior
     without having to assume a theory of the unconscious
     and repression. The alternative ways include such
     topics as automatic behavior, subliminal events,
     memory processes, self-deception, the unavailability
     of verbal labels, the incomplete assimilation of ex-
     perience, and forgetting. (Psycho-Personal
     Approach)

561. Patterson, Robert. "Death on the Mississippi: Mark Twain's Huckleberry Finn." Psychological Perspectives 7, no. 1 (Spr 1976): 9-22. Patterson analyzes the real and allegorical deaths in Huckleberry Finn according to Jung's theory of archetypes and the unconscious. (Transpersonal-Spiritual Approach)

562. Paul, D. Y. "The structure of consciousness in Paramartha's purported trilogy." Philosophy East and West (Jul 1981). One part of the structure involves what Paul called the "subconscious clearinghouse" ("alayavijnana") for karmic "seeds." "Seed" refers to psychic traces of some act. These seeds influence one's behavior in subtle ways. Spiritual freedom, indeed salvation, involves the discovery and elimination of these subconscious influences until one reaches a seedless state of consciousness. (Psycho-Personal Approach)

563. Payne, William Osborn. An Unconscious Autobiography. New York: Private printing, 1938. This work includes the diary and letters of W. O. Payne from 1796-1804.

564. Pedersen, Loren E. "An empirical demonstration of the shadow archetype, utilizing an imagery method." Ph.D. dissertation, California School of Professional Psychology, San Francisco, 1975. Pederson attempts to give construct validity to the Jungian notion of the shadow archetype. The technique used is the "unconscious mind mirror" imagery technique borrowed from Eric Greenleaf. See also Eric Greenleaf.

565. Peinado, Altable, and Sanchez Jaen. Psicoligía pedagógica. Lo subconsciente y la educación. (Pedagogical psychology. The subconscious and education.) Madrid: M. Aguilar, 1932. A psychoanalytical point of view is assumed with special focus on the ideas of Freud, Jung, and others.

566. Perry, J. "The messianic hero." Journal of Analytical Psychology 17, no. 2 (1972): 184-98. Perry is attempting to address the phenomenon and problem of psychic inflation by offering a translation

program to better handle inflationary material aris-
ing from the unconscious. For example, a messianic image is interpreted as a psychic push for
personal inner transformation and not as a mandate
to be a messiah.

567.   Perwin, Cynthia L. "The ego, the self, and the
        structure of political authority." Ph.D. disserta-
        tion, Princeton University, 1976. This study cen-
        ters on Thomas Hobbes' Leviathan. Perwin, using
        the ideas of Freud, Jung, Wittgenstein, and others,
        attempts to demonstrate the significance of the
        reality of the unconscious vis-à-vis political theory.

568.   Peters, J. A. J. "Wijgerige benzinning op het 'onbe-
        wuste'." (Philosophical reflection on the uncon-
        scious.) Gawein 12, no. 4 (1964): 245-56. This
        is a philosophical discussion of the roles of knowing
        and of awareness. The Freudian unconscious is
        discussed, but the point is made that the uncon-
        scious need not be considered an independent entity.
        A person is not just "self" conscious nor just an
        unconscious corporality, but a "self" that unifies
        one's experiences. (Psycho-Personal Approach)

569.   Petri, O. Nei profondi dominii dello spirito. Il
        Messia trascendentale. (In the deep fields of the
        spirit. The transcendental Messiah.) Rome:
        Maglione, 1931. In this book Petri uses the term
        "subconscious," which he defines as the reserve
        of experiences that the neurons have fixed in time
        and space. Some of the topics he discusses in-
        clude limitations of our spirit, Freudism, humani-
        ty's position in the universe, laws of causality,
        intelligence of the state, mechanism of volition,
        and so forth.

570.   Pfister, Oskar. "Sünde und Herzensreinheit im Lichte
        der Tiefenseelsorge." (Sin and innocence from the
        point of view of therapy of the unconscious.)
        Zeitschrift für Religiouspsychologie 1 (1928): 5-27.
        The author makes a case for how analysis can help
        in the mediation of salvation. The focus is on the
        conquest of sin and the process of purification.
        (Psycho-Personal Approach)

571.   _____. "Die Rolles des Unbewussten im philoso-
        phischen Denken." (The role of the unconscious

in philosophical thinking.) <u>Dialectica</u> 3 (1949): 254-71.

572. Phillips, W. "The subconsciousness and the acquirement of a second language. Conditions of most effective work. Part II." <u>Forum of Education</u> 8 (1930): 135-42. It is contended that the subconscious can facilitate the acquisition of a new language. (Psycho-Personal Approach)

573. Pi Süner, A. "Chimie, innervation et subconscient." (Chemistry, innervation, and the subconscious.) <u>La Psychologie et la vie</u> 6 (1932): 14-16. The author discusses the chemical foundation of the subconscious. (Bio-Physical Approach)

574. Piaget, Jean. "The affective unconscious and the cognitive unconscious." <u>Journal of American Psychoanalytic Association</u> 21 (1973): 249-61. Piaget compares and contrasts the cognitive unconscious with the Freudian affective unconscious. Essentially he is saying that there is an unconscious that is the function of cognitive processes just as there is an unconscious which is the function of emotive factors. The two types are distinct but mutually influence each other. (Psycho-Personal Approach)

575. Piccinino, F. "L'incosciente. In cerca del divino nelle manifestazioni della mente umana." (The unconscious. In search for the divine in the human mind.) <u>Gazzetta Internazionale di medicina e chirurgia</u> no. 2-3 (1930): 49-51, 74-88.

576. Pichon, E. "Observations sur le travail de M. Velikovsky." (Observations on the paper of M. Velikovsky.) <u>Revue française de psychanalyse</u> 10, no. 1 (1938). Pichon contends that Velikovsky did not show that the unconscious thought of Jews newly immigrated to Palestine is effected in Hebrew. (Psycho-Personal Approach)

577. _____. ["Note to reconcile an apparent contradiction."] <u>Revue française de psychanalyse</u> 10, no. 2 (1938). Pichon draws a distinction between the unconscious level below the sphere of language (the Freudian unconscious) and the preconscious where thoughts related to language are elaborated. (Psycho-Personal Approach)

578. Pierce, B. "The subconscious factor in medicine."
Lancet 213 (1927): 1221-25. Pierce evaluates the
use of Freudian concepts in medicine and finds
them suggestive at best and in need of a better
scientific foundation. The idea of the subconscious,
though, is useful. (Psycho-Personal Approach)

579. Pierce, F. Our Unconscious Mind and How to Use It.
New York: Dutton and Company, 1922. (Transpersonal-Spiritual Approach)

580. Pierce, Russell A. "The correspondence between
astrological motifs and Jungian archetypes." Ph.D.
dissertation, California School of Professional
Psychology, San Diego, 1976. It is suggested that
astrology is in part a projection of the collective
unconscious and as such can be very useful to the
student of human behavior. (Transpersonal-
Spiritual Approach)

581. Pike, Alfred. "The theory of unconscious perception
in music: A phenomenological criticism." Journal
of Aesthetics and Art Criticism 25, no. 4 (1967):
395-400. Pike is attempting to refute the ideas of
Anton Ehrenzweig. See also Anton Ehrenzweig.

582. Placci, C. "Divagazioni psicologiche." (Psychological
divagations.) Nuova antologia 65 (1930): 472-76.
The author contends that the manifestations, re-
juvenations, and diversifications in fine art, philosophy, religion, and politics have their causes in
the unconscious.

583. Pohl, Jan. ["The function of the synergism of con-
sciousness and unconsciousness in the dream."]
Dynamische Psychiatrie 12, no. 5 (1979): 395-405.
The ideas of G. Ammon are presented and discussed.

584. Pongratz, Ludwig J. "Das Logogramm der Psychologie." (The logogram of psychology.) Jahrbuch für
Psychologie, Psychotherapie und medizinische An-
thropologie 15, no. 1-2 (Jan 1967): 67-76. Pongratz suggests a logogram of the mutual interaction
of four aspects of a person's life, such as the
conscious, the unconscious, feelings, and behavior.
(Psycho-Personal Approach)

585. Ponomarev, Ya A. "Vzaimootnoshenie priamogo (osoz-
     navaemogo) i pobochnogo (neosoznavaemogo) produk-
     tov deistviia." [The interrelationship of direct
     (conscious) products of action and its (unconscious)
     by-products.] Voprosy Psikhologii 5, no. 4 (1959):
     90-104.

586. Powell, R. C. "The 'subliminal' versus the 'subcon-
     scious' in the American acceptance of psychoanaly-
     sis, 1906-1910." Journal of the History of Be-
     havioral Science 15, no. 2 (Apr 1979): 155-65.
     This is a discussion of F. W. H. Myers' and the
     Emmanuel Movement's influence toward the accept-
     ance of Freudian ideas in America.

587. Prangishvili, A. S. "The problem of the unconscious
     in the psychological concept of set." Soviet Psy-
     chology 20, no. 3 (Spr 1982): 24-35.

588. _____; A. E. Sherozia; and F. V. Bassin, eds.
     The Unconscious: Nature, Functions, Methods of
     Study, Volumes 1-3. Tbilisis, USSR: Metsniereba,
     1978. (Bio-Physical and Psycho-Personal
     Approaches)

589. Prasad, J. "The conscious, the sub-conscious, and
     the unconscious." Indian Journal of Psychology 4
     (1929): 72-88. The authors conducts a critical
     analysis of what the terms mean. (Psycho-Personal
     Approach)

590. Prasad, K. "A Gestalt approach to the concept of the
     unconscious." Philosophical Quarterly 8 (1932):
     227-41. Prasad discusses the Freudian understand-
     ing of conscious, preconscious, and unconscious in
     terms of the construct of "fusion-wholes." (Psycho-
     Personal Approach)

591. Pratt, E. B. "The role of the unconscious in The
     Eternal Husband." Literature and Psychology 22,
     no. 1 (1972): 13-25. Fyodor Dostoevsky's novel
     is discussed as an example of how the unconscious
     helps someone cope with life's pressures. (Psycho-
     Personal Approach)

592. Price, H. "Some philosophical questions about telepathy
     and clairvoyance." Philosophy 15 (1940): 363-85.

Price wants to assume that telepathic and clairvoy-
ant experiences do happen and proceeds to offer
some possible explanations for these events. One
of the possibilities involves what he refers to as
"omnisentient consciousness," which is similar to
the notion of "World-Soul" or "collective unconscious." He also argues that the answer to what
the unconscious is involves more than merely trying
to decide if it is mental or physiological in nature.
He suggests that it could involve some third category. (Transpersonal-Spiritual Approach)

593. Prince, Morton. The Unconscious. New York: Macmillan, 1929. Prince's ideas about the unconscious
are based on his theory of neurograms or neuro-
graphic residua of experiences. The unconscious
is the storehouse of these neurograms. In his
model of the psyche Prince subdivides the subconscious into two dimensions: the co-conscious and
the unconscious. (Bio-Physical and Psycho-Personal
Approaches)

594. Progoff, Ira. Death and Rebirth of Psychology. New
York: Julian Press, 1956. Among other topics
Progoff discusses the significance of the psychology
of the unconscious for the twentieth century person.

595. _____. "Psychology as a road to a personal philosophy." Journal of Individual Psychology 17 (1961):
43-48. The road to a personal philosophy is often-
times facilitated by the influences of the unconscious.

596. _____. Jung, Synchronicity, and Human Destiny.
New York: Dell Publishing Company, Inc., 1973.
This work centers on Jung's theory of the collective
unconscious. (Transpersonal-Spiritual Approach)

597. Pulver, Sidney. "Can affects be unconscious?" International Journal of Psychoanalysis 52 (1971):
347-54. Pulver contends that affects can be unconscious and cites a case in point which involves both
hypnotism and automatic writing. The case is
highly suggestive at best. (Psycho-Personal Approach)

598. _____. "Unconscious versus potential affects."
Psychoanalytic Quarterly 43, no. 1 (1974): 77-84.

Pulver distinguishes unconscious affects which are items of mental content, and potential affects which are structural dispositions to produce affects. Both modes influence behavior without the person being aware of it. (Bio-Physical and Psycho-Personal Approaches)

599. Rabinowitz, Aaron. "Reflections on the concept of the unconscious in Judaism." Journal of Psychology and Judaism 4, no. 1 (1979): 49-57. The question addressed is whether the concept of the unconscious is congruent or alien to Jewish thought. Some feel that the concept is alien because it can be used to espouse a personal responsibility-denying determinism. Rabinowitz does not think that this is the case and argues that the concept is congruent with Judaism. (Psycho-Personal Approach)

600. Rabkin, R. "Is the unconscious necessary?" International Journal of Psychiatry (1969): 570-78.

601. Radil, T.; J. Radilova; V. Bozkov; and Z. Bohdanecky. "Unconscious and conscious processes during visual perception." Acta Neurobiologieae Experimentalis 41, no. 6 (1981): 565-72.

602. Rado, Sandor. "Mind, unconscious mind, and brain." In Psychoanalysis of Behavior, pp. 180-85. New York: Grune & Stratton, 1956. Rado is essentially a Freudian except that he prefers to substitute for the construct of the unconscious the expression "nonreporting sector or level." The unconscious mind is merely a "nonreporting organization of causative links between processes of which we are aware" (pp. 181-2). Rado is very concerned to avoid any metaphysical entanglements. (Psycho-Personal Approach)

603. Raffe, Deena. "Competitive behavior in women: The influence of unconscious factors." Ph.D. dissertation, Northwestern University, 1980. This experimental study involves the use of subliminally presented material to forty-eight females and forty-eight males. (Bio-Physical and Psycho-Personal Approaches)

604. Ramirez, Augustine. "Unconscious drives and human freedom in Freud's psychoanalysis." Ph.D. dis-

sertation, Catholic University of American, 1955.
(Psycho-Personal Approach)

605. Ramus, C. Behind the Scenes with Ourselves. New
York: Century, 1931. Ramus expounds on a model
of the psyche that includes the personal subconscious, the conscious consciousness, and the super-
conscious self. The first is selfish, the second is
our everyday waking state, and the third is altru-
istic. (Transpersonal-Spiritual Approach)

606. Rank, Otto. The Trauma of Birth. New York: Robert
Brunner, 1952. Rank puts forth his theory of the
significance of the birth trauma, its repression,
and its influence on a person's psychic development.
The unconscious has its beginning in the birth
trauma, is essentially a repressed unconscious, and
is ever active in a person's life. Sometimes Rank
implies that the Unconscious is a kind of "second
self" or some "It." (Psycho-Personal Approach)

607. Ranschburg, P. "Beiträge zum Verhalten der Reflexe,
Automatismen und bewussten Funktionen in scheinbar
unbewussten Zuständen." (Contributions to the study
of the action of reflexes, automatisms and conscious
functions in apparently unconscious states.) Zeitschrift für Psychologie 129 (1933): 338-52. The
author argues for a theory of continuous gradations
of consciousness from merely conscious (without
self-consciousness) to fully self-conscious state.
The study is supported by case reports of narcoti-
zation and its effects.

608. Rappaport, B. "Carnal knowledge: What the wisdom
of the body has to offer psychotherapy." Journal
of Humanistic Psychology 15, no. 1 (Win 1975):
49-70. The theme of this article is "you are your
body." Rappaport reviews the various body thera-
pies such as Rolfing, polarity therapy, Alexander
technique, yoga, sensory awareness, aikido, dance,
and t'ai chi chuan. What is relevant to the topic
of the unconscious is that sometimes the "wisdom
of the body" is talked about in terms of some unconscious that is the agent behind such wisdom.
(Bio-Physical Approach)

609. Rauhala, Lauri. "Intentionality and the problem of the
unconscious." Annales Universitatis Turkuensis,

Series B 110 (1969). Rauhala conducts a philosophical discussion of the fundamental problems regarding the unconscious. Such problems include the
question of what the term means, its relationship
to conceptions of the human, and the philosophical
foundation needed to unify the different approaches
regarding the unconscious. Rauhala also features
the ideas of Carl Jung.

610. Rawcliffe, D. H. "The subconscious mind." In Illu-
sions and Delusions of the Supernatural and the Occult, pp. 26-31. New York: Dover Publications,
1959. Rawcliffe uses a theory of the subconscious
to explain occult and supernatural experiences.
For him the subconscious mind is a collective term
for all mental activity occurring below the level of
consciousness. Ironically Rawcliffe creates as much
mystery with his notion of the subconscious as he
tried to dispel with the same notion. The book is
an interesting exercise in rationalization. (Psycho-
Personal Approach)

611. Raymond, G. L. The Psychology of Inspiration. New
York: Funk & Wagnalls, 1908. The author employs
a construct of the subconscious to attempt to understand the phenomenon of inspiration.

612. Rayner, E. "Infinite experiences, affects and the
characteristics of the unconscious." International
Journal of Psychoanalysis 62, part 4 (1981): 403-12.
This is a discussion of I. Matte-Blanco's use of
mathematical symbolic logic to elucidate psychoanalytical concepts. Rayner points out that asym-
metrical logic is analogous to secondary process
while symmetrical logic is characteristic of primary
processes. (Psycho-Personal Approach)

613. Razran, G. "The observable unconscious and the in-
ferable conscious in current Soviet psychophysiolo-
gy." Psychological Review 68 (1961): 81-147. The
title is misleading here. Razran is thoroughly
grounded in a bio-physical approach regarding the
unconscious. His article is all about developments
in interoceptive conditioning, semantic conditioning,
and orienting reflex. What he means by "observable" is the fact that the experimenter can measure
the degree of interoceptive response by some physical
parameter, such as secretions.

614. Reidy, Mary E. "A study of the unconscious effect of
approval and disapproval on verbal behavior."
Ph. D. dissertation, Catholic University of America,
1958. (Psycho-Personal Approach)

615. Reik, T. Der überraschte Psychologie. Über Erraten
und Verstehen unbewusster Vorgänge. (The aston-
ished psychologist. On the apprehension and com-
prehension of unconscious processes.) Leiden:
Sijthoff, 1935.

616. Rendon, M. "Structuralism in psychoanalysis." American Journal of Psychoanalysis 39, no. 4 (1979):
343-51. Rendon refers to Lévi-Strauss and Piaget,
both of whom defined the unconscious as the lack of
awareness of mechanisms influencing group and individual behavior. This adjectival usage of the term
differs from Freud's, who used the noun form of
the word and referred to a psychic subsystem of
repressed material. (Psycho-Personal Approach)

617. Revesz, G. "De verhouding van de taal tot het onbewuste en de droom." (The correlation between
language, the unconscious, and dreaming.) Nederlandsch tijdschrift voor psychologie 6 (1951): 201-8.

618. Rhine, J. B. "On the nature and consequences of the
unconsciousness of psi." Journal of Parapsychology
22 (1958): 175-86. Rhine discusses the difficulty
of control over ESP phenomena because of the unawareness connected to its operations.

619. Ribot, Théodule A. La Vie Inconsciente e les Mouve-
ments. (Unconscious life and movements.) Paris:
Alcan, 1914. The author uses the term "subcon-
consciousness."

620. Richardson, William. "The place of the unconscious
in Heidegger." Review of Existential Psychology
and Psychiatry 5, no. 3 (1965): 265-90. The author is relating the Freudian unconscious to the
ideas of Heidegger. (Psycho-Personal Approach)

621. Rieff, Phillip. "The hidden self." In Freud: The
Mind of the Moralist, pp. 65-101. New York: The
Viking Press, 1959. The notion of "hidden self"
is closely related to the construct of the unconscious. (Psycho-Personal Approach)

622. Riha, Sonia A. "The unconscious and symbolic imagery." Ph.D. dissertation, California School of
Professional Psychology, 1972. Riha acknowledges
that the unconscious is a real influence on behavior
and proceeds to present and compare four methods
of gaining access to unconscious material. The
four "roads" to the unconscious include Hedda
Bolgar's waking dream technique, Carl Jung's active imagination method practiced by Harold Stone,
Desoille's guided or directed daydream technique,
and Robert Resnicke's Gestalt dreamwork method.
(Psycho-Personal Approach)

623. Ring, Kenneth. "A transpersonal view of consciousness: A mapping of farther regions of inner
space." Journal of Transpersonal Psychology 2
(1974): 125-55. Ring outlines his map of the psyche
which includes the following: pre-conscious, psychodynamic unconscious, ontogenetic unconscious,
phylogenetic unconscious, trans-individual unconscious, extraterrestrial unconscious, superconscious,
and the Void. (Transpersonal-Spiritual Approach)

624. _____. "Mapping the regions of consciousness: A
conceptual reformulation." Journal of Transpersonal
Psychology 8, no. 2 (1976): 77-88. This is really
a re-mapping of his 1974 picture of the psyche. He
literally draws a new map using a circular diagram.
Ring's understanding of the unconscious spans all four
approaches. (Transpersonal-Spiritual Approach)

625. Ringel, E., and W. Spiel. "Zur Problematik des Unbewussten vom Standpunkt der Individualpsychologie."
(On the problem of the unconscious from the point
of view of individual psychology.) Psyche 6 (1952):
378-88. (Psycho-Personal Approach)

626. Rivers, W. H. R. Instinct and the Unconscious. London: Cambridge University Press, 1924. The unconscious is understood to refer to experiences
that cannot be brought into consciousness by any of
the usual processes of memory or association, but
require special techniques or states such as sleep,
hypnotism, free association, and so forth in order
to retrieve the memories. (Psycho-Personal Approach)

627. Robbins, Lewis L. "Unconscious motivation." Menninger Quarterly 10, no. 2 (1956): 24-28. Robbins

discusses the evidence for the existence of the unconscious and the unconscious' influence on behavior. (Psycho-Personal Approach)

628. Rochon-Duvigneaud, A. "Emotion provoquée par un souvenir inconscient." (Emotion caused by an unconscious remembrance.) Journal de Psychologie Normale et Pathologique 33 (1936): 283-85. This is an autobiographical account of discovering the unremembered reason for certain reactions to the sight of a flower. (Psycho-Personal Approach)

629. Rollins, Nancy. "The new Soviet approach to the unconscious." American Journal of Psychiatry 131, no. 3 (1974): 301-4. Rollins discusses the notion of "set" as a key concept toward the understanding of the unconscious. (Bio-Physical and Psycho-Personal Approaches)

630. _____. "A Soviet study of consciousness and unconsciousness." Journal of Individual Psychology 31, no. 2 (1975): 230-38. Rollins reviews F. V. Bassin's book The Problem of the Unconscious. She also discusses the notion of "set," and comments on the shift in Soviet thought from a sociogenic conception of psychiatric illness to a more intra-psychic understanding. (Bio-Physical and Psycho-Personal Approaches)

631. _____. "Consciousness, unconsciousness, and the concept of repression." In The Unconscious: Nature, Functions, Methods of Study, Vol. 1. Edited by A. Prangishvili, A. Sherozia, and F. Bassin. Tbilisi, USSR: Metsniereba, 1978. (Bio-Physical and Psycho-Personal Approaches)

632. Romano, P. ["Some considerations on Jungian psychology as a topical question in the current cultural situation."] Rivista Sperimentale di Freniatria e Medicina Legale delle Alienazioni Mentali 96, no. 5 (Oct 1972): 1381-89. Romano discusses the influence of both personal and collective unconscious in personal development. He contends that a psychology of the collective unconscious facilitates the development of a mature dependency on others.

633. Romanyshyn, Robert D. "Phenomenology and psychoanalysis: Contributions of Merleau-Ponty." Psy-

choanalytic Review 64, no. 2 (1977): 211-23. According to Romanyshyn, Merleau-Ponty understood
an unconscious that refers to the immediacy of experience. As such this approach toward the unconscious does not fit neatly into any of the four categories of the typology outlined in the Introduction
of this bibliography.

634. Rosenfeld, Eduard. The Book of the Highs. New
York: Quadrangle, 1973. The author surveys 250
methods to alter consciousness. Some of the methods discussed involve the use of the construct of
the unconscious.

635. Rosenfield, Israel. "A study of Freud's theory of
unconscious motives." Ph.D. dissertation. Princeton University, 1966. Rosenfield evaluates Freud's
contribution to sociology and finds it questionable
because Freud failed to attribute any verbal content
to the unconscious. Without such content it is difficult to speak of unconscious motivation and still
more difficult to speak of archaic heritages. Rosenfield contends that Freud's theory of the unconscious is grounded in physiology and as such is
legitimate but not appropriate in trying to understand the psychological question of motivation.
(Bio-Physical and Psycho-Personal Approaches)

636. _____. Character and Consciousness: A Study of
Freud's Theory of Unconscious Motives. New York:
University Books, 1970. (Psycho-Personal
Approach)

637. Rosenzweig, Saul. "The cultural matrix of the unconscious." American Psychologist 7, no. 10 (1956):
561-62. This short piece is a historical analysis
of the cultural factors out of which Freud emerged
with his theory of the unconscious. (Psycho-
Personal Approach)

638. Rosicrucians. "Your other selves ... Awaken the psychic you." Science Digest (Feb 1982): 116. An
advertisement. (Transpersonal-Spiritual Approach)

639. Rosinska, Zofia. "Antropologia analityczna Junga a
humanizm." (Jung's analytic anthropology and
humanism.) Studia Filozoficzne Supplement (1969):
249-58. There is a discussion of the collective

unconscious and its role in individuation and the
creative process. (Transpersonal-Spiritual
Approach)

640. Rossi, Ernest L. "As above, so below: the holographic mind." Psychological Perspective 11, no. 2
(Fall 1980): 155-69. Rossi maintains that holo-
graphy can be the unifying principle for integrating
our understanding of the mental and the physical.
He suggests that maybe the collective unconscious
operates according to holographic principles and
that this could be the foundation for synchronistic
and parapsychological events. (Transpersonal-
Spiritual Approach)

641. Rossi, Ino. "The unconscious in the anthropology of
Claude Levi-Strauss." American Anthropologist
75, no. 1 (1973): 20-48. For Lévi-Strauss the
unconscious represents the aggregate of certain
infra-structures (logical and anatomical) that determine mental functioning, and ultimately cultural
phenomena (superstructures). Knowing these structures can serve to better understand customs, in-
stitutions, and other social aspects.

642. _____, ed. The Unconscious in Culture. New York:
E. P. Dutton, 1974. This book deals with the anthropology of Claude Lévi-Strauss.

643. Roth, Robert J., ed. "Bifurcated psyche and social
self: Implications of Freud's theory of the unconscious." In Person and Community, pp. 43-62.
New York: Fordham University Press, 1975.
(Psycho-Personal Approach)

644. Rothenhäusler, O. "Charakterologische Kriterien zur
Psychopathologie." (Characterological criteria in
psychopathology.) Zeitschrift für die gesamte
Neurologie und Psychiatrie 112 (1928): 275-78.
The author discusses abnormal personalities in
terms of the "forcible entry of the unconsious" and
domination of the unconscious. A repressed unconscious is assumed here. (Psycho-Personal
Approach)

645. Rothgeb, Carrie L., ed. Abstracts of the Collected
Works of C. G. Jung and Abstracts of the Standard

Edition of the Complete Psychological Works of
Sigmund Freud. Washington, D.C.: U.S. Govern-
ment Printing Office, 1978. (See S. Freud and C.
Jung.)

646. Rotthaus, Erich. "Ergänzende Bemerkungen über die
Willensfreiheit und die Hierarchie des Unbewussten. "
(Supplementary notes on free will and the hierarchy
of the unconscious.) Jahrbuch für Psychologie und
Psychotherapie 3 (1955): 327-31. It seems that
Rotthaus is referring to conscious when he writes
about the unconscious.

647. Rubin, T. I. Through My Own Eyes (An Awakened
Unconscious). New York: Macmillan, 1982. This
autobiographical account features no discussion of
the unconscious per se.

648. Rucker, N. G., and C. B. Mermelstein. "Unconscious
communication in the mother-child dyad. " American
Journal of Psychoanalysis 39, no. 2 (Sum 1979):
147-51. (Psycho-Personal Approach)

649. Sabini, M. Review of the religious images in the motion pictures "Star Wars, " "Close Encounters of
the Third Kind, " and "Oh, God. " Quadrant (Win
1978): 105-110. These movies are interpreted as
if they were the dreams of the collective unconscious
of a culture. (Socio-Cultural Approach)

650. Sabnis, G. K. "The Unconscious through the ages. "
Bombay University Journal 4, part 4 and 6 (1936):
91-133, 102-138. Sabnis does a brief history of
the idea of the unconscious leading up to and in-
cluding Freud. Sabnis coins the expression "unconsciousism. " He writes about the "Innate unconscious, " the "Acquired unconscious, " the "Freudian unconscious, " and the "Metaphysical unconscious. " He also refers to Montmasson's notion
of the "distant" or palingenetic" unconscious.

651. Sachs, H. Creative Unconscious. Cambridge, Mass.:
Sci-Art Publishers, 1951. This book features a
psychoanalytic approach to art expressions. (Psycho-
Personal Approach)

652. Sadler, W. S. The Mind at Mischief. New York:
Funk & Wagnalls, 1929. Sadler, drawing on the

ideas of Freud, Jung, and Adler, discusses such
things as the subconscious, defense mechanisms,
and a variety of parapsychological phenomena.

653. Sampson, Harold. "A critique of certain traditional
concepts in the psychoanalytic theory of therapy."
Bulletin of the Menninger Clinic 40, no. 3 (May
1976): 255-62. Sampson contrasts his "control
mastery theory" with psychoanalytic theories. He
argues that one can exercise some control over the
unconscious. The unconscious is not totally autonomous. (Psycho-Personal Approach)

654. Sandler, Joseph. "Dreams, unconscious fantasies and
'identity of perception'." International Review of
Psycho-Analysis 3, no. 1 (1976): 33-42. Working
within the Freudian system of ideas, Sandler attempts to explain how instinctual wishes can be
fulfilled and still protect consciousness. (Psycho-
Personal Approach)

655. _____. "Unconscious wishes and human relationships." Contemporary Psychoanalysis 17, no. 2
(Apr 1981): 180-96. (Psycho-Personal Approach)

656. _____. "Unbewusste Wunsche und menschliche
Beziehungen." (Subconscious wishes and human
relations.) Psyche 36, no. 1 (Jan 1982): 59-74.
(Psycho-Personal Approach)

657. _____; Alex Holder; and Christopher Dare. "Frames
of reference in psychoanalytic psychology: VI.
The topographical frame of reference: The unconscious." British Journal of Medical Psychology
46, no. 1 (Mar 1973): 37-43. The authors focus
on such topics as the pleasure-pain principle and
the characteristics of primary processes. (Psycho-
Personal Approach)

658. Sanford, A. The Healing Light. St. Paul, Minn.:
Macalester Park Publishing Company, 1947. In
discussing the art of healing the author alludes to
the subconscious as part of the healing process.
(Transpersonal-Spiritual Approach)

659. Sapir, Edward. "The unconscious patterning of behavior
in society." In The Unconscious, A Symposium,

pp. 114-42. Edited by C. M. Child, New York:
Alfred A. Knopf, 1927. Sapir argues that much of
our social behavior is a matter of naive practice
rather than behavior we could consciously describe.
He rejects any tendency to reify the construct of
the unconscious. (Psycho-Personal Approach)

660. Sartre, Jean-Paul. "Bad faith." In Being and Nothing-
ness, pp. 47-54. New York: Philosophical Library, Inc., 1956. Sartre criticizes Freud for
splitting the psyche into two by his theory of the
unconscious. Sartre finds theoretical problems
with the assumption of the unconscious. He would
rather consider the person and psyche as one and
argue that the person does not want to know about
certain aspects of behavior rather than say that the
person does not know because of repression. Sartre
reasons that the person must know that which needs
to be repressed and hence the notion of bad faith.
(Psycho-Personal Approach)

661. Saturday Review. "Mind and SuperMind." (Feb. 22,
1975): 10-34.

662. Satya Nand, D. The Findings of Soul-Analysis (total
psychoanalysis). Old Delhi, India: D. Satya Nand,
1951. The author contrasts the ideas of Jung,
Stekel, McDougall, and Freud with soul-analysis.
This work represents another point of interface
between Occidental and Oriental thinking about the
unconscious. Satya Nand devotes some attention
to the notion of "racial mind."

663. Saunders, Brian S. "Melville's inland imagination:
Idealism and the unconscious in 'Redburn' and
'Pierre'." Ph.D. dissertation, Cornell University,
1981.

664. Saxe, Doreen. "Twentieth-Century studies of Racine
and the unconscious." Ph.D. dissertation, University of North Carolina at Chapel Hill, 1972. This
works features three key things: 1) a historical
account of the concept of the unconscious up through
Freud and his successors with particular reference
to the art; 2) the unconscious aspects of artistic
creation as understood by C. Baudouin, C. Mauron,
F. Lion, J. Starobinski, and R. Barthes; and 3)

a study of the unconscious aspects of Racine's works as informed by the previous two considerations.

665.   Schairer, I. B. Die Nacht des Unbewussten und die Macht des Christentums. (The night of the unconscious and the might of Christianity.) Stuttgart: Steinkopf, 1927.

666.   Schimek, Jean G. "A critical re-examination of Freud's concept of unconscious mental representation." International Review of Psycho-Analysis 2 (1975): 171ff. Schimek argues against the idea that the unconscious is a storage container of specific images and memories. He contends that the unconscious has more to do with subtle sensori-motor organizers of action at a pre-ideational level. (Bio-Physical and Psycho-Personal Approaches)

667.   Schmidbauer, W. "Das Unbewusste und das Kind." (The unconscious and the child.) Ther Ggw 118, no. 12 (Dec 1979): 1783-97.

668.   Schneck, Jerome M. "Blushing and unconscious hostility." Diseases of the Nervous System 28, no. 10 (1967): 679. A journal summary. (Psycho-Personal Approach)

669.   Schneider, Ernst. "Zur Psychologie des Unbewussten." (About the psychology of the unconscious.) Schweizerische Zeitschrift für Psychologie und ihre Anwendungen 11 (1952): 99-120. Schneider writes about the soul as that which orchestrates both conscious and unconscious activities. He discusses the "instinctive unconscious" which both controls the development of the physical body and is the foundation for primordial images, such as Jung's archetypes.

670.   Schnier, Jacques. "Art symbolism and the unconscious." Journal of Aesthetics 12 (1953): 67-75. The author takes a psychoanalytical point of view to do a multi-cultural study of the relationship between ships and burial scenes in art. (Psycho-Personal Approach)

671.   Schnitzer, Robert D. "Personal adjustment and the recognition and unconscious evaluation of self-

expressive forms. " Ph.D. dissertation, Brandeis
University, 1961. (Psycho-Personal Approach)

672. Schuurman, C. J. De taal van het onbewuste zieleleven.
(The language of the unconscious inner life.) Arn-
hem: Van Loghum Slaterus, 1951. The focus here
is on the unconscious sources of fairy tales, art
and reality, illness and crime, myth, the dream,
and fantasy.

673. Scolastico, Ronald B. "Meaningful communication and
the unconscious: The contribution of humanistic
psychology. " Ph.D. dissertation, University of
Iowa, 1978. Essentially the author is arguing
against the negative, disruptive model of the unconscious in favor of a positive, growth-orientated
model. Humanistic psychologists ask about what
the unconscious is trying to unfold and not what it
is trying to hide. (Psycho-Personal Approach)

674. Scripture, W. E. "Ein Einblick in den unbewussten
Versmechanismus. " (A glimpse into the unconscious verse mechanism.) Zeitschrift für Psychologie 102 (1927): 307-9. Scripture presents an
example of how the unconscious is superior to consciousness in translating poetic verses. He also
points out that the unconscious verse mechanism is
very important to poets and writers.

675. Secco-Bellati, Myrta. ["A problem of the archaic
superego: Interference. "] Etudes Psychotherapiques
no. 26 (Dec 1976): 239-45. A case study is presented showing how the guided daydream technique
can facilitate the recovery of unconscious archaic
fantasies.

676. Seeley, J. R. "The Americanization of the unconscious. " Atlantic 208, no. 1 (1962): 68ff.

677. Seidmann, P. "The capacity for 'sentient listening':
Anthropological reflections on a postulate of depth
psychology. " Psychotherapy and Psychosomatics
22, no. 1 (1973): 52-64. Seidmann contends that
sentient listening for the repressed unconscious
is an essential psychotherapeutic skill and that
Freud was the first to recognize the necessity of
such a skill. (Psycho-Personal Approach)

678. Seligman, C. G. "The unconscious in relation to anthropology." British Journal of Psychology 18, part 4 (1928): 373-87. Seligman maintains that the psychology of the unconscious can help solve some of the problems in anthropology such as how to account for similiar forms of expression among different groups of people especially when the possibility of physical transmission is unlikely. Essentially he is suggesting that there may exist one commonly held human race unconscious. (Socio-Cultural Approach)

679. Serota, Herman M. "The ego and the unconscious: 1784-1884." Psychoanalytic Quarterly 43, no. 2 (1974): 224-42. Serota discusses the sources of Freud's concepts of ego and unconscious in literature published between 1784-1884. (Psycho-Personal Approach)

680. Sevier, Marcus W. "Adventures of the ego in the unconscious: A Jungian analysis of the unspelling group of Sir Gawain poems in Middle English." Ph.D. dissertation, University of Texas at Austin, 1978. Each poem is interpreted as being expressive in symbolic form of one phase in the individuation process; that is, coming to terms with aspects of one's unconscious.

681. Shadkow, D. The Influence of Freud on American Psychology. New York: International Universities Press, 1964. Shakow discusses how the psychology of the unconscious impacted American psychology. (Psycho-Personal Approach)

682. Shalev, Sara. "The unconscious as a healer." Confinia Psychiatrica 21, no. 1-3 (1978): 150-55. This is a case study of a woman who experienced therapeutic insight through contact with the unconscious. Paintings and drawings were used in the process. (Psycho-Personal Approach)

683. Shalvey, T. Claude Lévi-Strauss: Social Psychotherapy and the Collective Unconscious. Amherst: University of Massachusetts Press, 1979.

684. Shapiro, David L. "The significance of the visual image in psychotherapy." Psychotherapy: Theory,

Research & Practice 7, no. 4 (Win 1970): 209-12. Shapiro discusses imagery as a direct representation of the unconscious. The unconscious is understood as the realm or system of subtle impulses seeking expression. In a sense the visual image is treated as another "road" to the unconscious. (Psycho-Personal Approach)

685. Sharma, A. K. "The psychological basis of autosuggestion." Monist 37 (1927): 404-21. According to Sharma the subconscious is that which can translate a suggestion into action through the power of imagination. (Psycho-Personal Approach)

686. Shastri, D. "The unconscious in Indian philosophy." Samiksa 22, no. 1 (1968): 33-41. This paper was read at the Symposium on the Unconscious held by the Indian Psycho-Analytical Society in Calcutta on February 11, 1968. Shastri admits that there is nothing in Indian philosophy that is equal to the Freudian unconscious. He does find some relationship with the notion of Karma and the idea of the unconscious as a storehouse of dispositions, drives, and so forth. He also makes mention of a "cosmic unconscious."

687. Shelburne, Walter A. "C. G. Jung's theory of the collective unconscious: A rational reconstruction." Ph.D. dissertation, University of Florida, 1976. The focus here is on the idea of the archetypes. After first attempting to elucidate what Jung meant by the archetypes Shelburne argues that the theory of archetypes can be considered scientific and compatible with standard scientific understanding. Shelburne also answers the charge of psychologism issued by J. Goldbrunner and M. Buber.

688. Shengold, Leonard, and James T. McLaughlin. "Plenary session on changes in psychoanalytic practice and experience: Theoretical, technical and social implications." International Journal of Psycho-Analysis 57, no. 3 (1976): 261-74. Among the many things discussed was the topic of "mystical unconscious communication."

689. Sheroziya, Apollon E. K probleme soznaniya i bessoznatel'nogo psikhicheskogo. (A contribution to the

problem of the conscious and the unconscious.)
Tbilisi, USSR: Metsnierebe, 1969. (Bio-Physical
and Psycho-Personal Approaches)

690. _____, and F. V. Bassin. "The results of the discussion and the prospects of a further study of the
problem of the unconscious." A paper delivered
at the International Symposium on the Problem of
the Unconscious. Tbilisi, USSR, 1979. The reality
and importance of the unconscious is acknowledged,
but beyond that there are differences of opinion regarding questions of terminology, methods, and
principles of interpretation. The paper also features a review of the state of the problem of the
unconscious in Russian psychology. The emphasis
is exclusively on bio-physical and psycho-personal
approaches. See item no. 41.

691. Shevach, David R. "Emotion and the unconscious."
Ph. D. dissertation, University of California, San
Diego, 1971. This is a philosophical-critical study
of the psychoanalytic theory of emotional conflict.
Shevach criticizes philosophers (Ryle, Malcolm,
and Austin) for writing off the unconscious as merely
a medical issue, and behaviorists for simply reducing symptoms to problems of conditioning. Then
Shevach argues that the distinction between conscious
and unconscious emotion has no topographical significance. It is a distinction between a disguised
form of expression such as a dream and a fully
verbalized form of expression. (Psycho-Personal
Approach)

692. Shevrin, Howard. "Rapaport's contribution to research." Bulletin of the Menninger Clinic 40, no.
1 (1976): 211-28. Shevrin makes the point that
all the necessary characteristics of psychological
functions can go on without the benefit of consciousness and hence the assumption of a psychological
unconscious is reasonable. The finding is based
on studies involving such things as subliminal
perception, binocular rivalry, attentional processes,
and so forth. (Bio-Physical Approach)

693. _____, and Scott Dickman. "The psychological unconscious, a necessary assumption for all psychological theory?" American Psychologist (May 1980):

421-33. The authors answer "yes" to the question.
They point out that complex cognitive activity can
go on without the benefit of consciousness. The
findings are based on studies in selective attention,
subliminal perception, cortical evoked potential,
and so forth. (Bio-Physical Approach)

694. _____, and Lester Luborsky. "The measurement
of preconscious perception in dreams and images:
An investigation of the Poetzl phenomenon." Journal of Abnormal Social Psychology 56 (1958): 285-
94. Findings tend to support Freud's assertion
that the neutral character of preconscious perception
permits it to serve as a cover for unconscious ideas
in order to pass censorship.

695. Shope, Robert K. "Freud on conscious and unconscious
intentions." Inquiry 13 (1970): 149-59. (Psycho-
Personal Approach)

696. Sidis, B. The Psychology of Suggestion. New York:
D. Appleton & Company, 1898. The subconscious
is discussed as one key factor in the phenomenon
of suggestion. (Psycho-Personal Approach)

697. Siegler, Frederick A. "Unconscious Intentions." Inquiry 10, no. 1 (Spr 1967): 251-67. (Psycho-
Personal Approach)

698. Sievers, W. D. Freud on Broadway. New York:
Hermitage Press, 1955. Sievers discusses the
relationship between the psychology of the unconscious (à la Freud) and the American drama.
(Psycho-Personal Approach)

699. Silverman, Lloyd H. "An experimental method for the
study of unconscious conflict: A progress report."
British Journal of Medical Psychology 48 (1975):
291-98. This experiment involves subliminally
received messages and their differential effect on
behavior. (Bio-Physical Approach)

700. Simon, F. B. "Die Evolution unbewusster Strukturen."
(Evolution of unconscious structures.) Psyche 37,
no. 6 (Jun 1983): 520-54. A psychoanalytical understanding of the unconscious is assumed. (Psycho-
Personal Approach)

701. Singer, June D. "Culture and the collective unconscious." Ph. D. dissertation, Northwestern University, 1968. Singer traces the historical sources
in anthropology and related fields for Jung's concept
of the collective unconscious. She makes the point
that "primitive man" and "civilized man" are not
two but one. They are united in the collective unconscious of each person. She suggests that knowing
of the reality of the collective unconscious can facilitate the arrival of world unity and peace.
(Socio-Cultural Approach)

702. _____. "A Jungian view of biofeedback training."
Journal of Transpersonal Psychology 8, no. 2
(1976): 112-18. Singer explains how biofeedback
can be understood as another way of approaching
the unconscious. She sees bio-feedback training as
a reflection on one level of the Jungian dictum of
the self-regulating power of the psyche.

703. Skinner, B. F. "A critique of psychoanalytic concepts
and theories." In Cumulative Record, pp. 185-94.
New York: Appleton-Century-Crofts, Inc., 1959.
Skinner expresses at length his criticisms of
Freudian ideas. Skinner finds no reason to enter-
tain a theory of the unconscious. For him patterns
of behavior, reinforcing contingencies, and learning
principles are sufficient to account for behavior.
(Bio-Physical Approach)

704. Smith, A. Art and the Subconscious. Maitland: Fla.:
Research Studio, 1937.

705. Soares Leites, Octavio. "Algumas críticas a noção de
inconsciente." (Some criticisms to the notion of
the unconscious.) Boletin del Instituto Psicologia,
Rio de Janeiro, 6, no. 3-4 (1956): 15-21. This
is a criticism of Freud's concept of the unconscious.
Sources of criticism come from logical positivists
who claim that the concept is meaningless, philosophers involved in language analysis who contend
that the term is meaningful but does not imply an
entity, and others who argue that the concept does
refer to an entity. (Psycho-Personal Approach)

706. Solomon, Robert C. "Unconscious motivation." Ph. D.
dissertation, University of Michigan, 1967. Solo-

mon's purpose is to provide a foundation for a philosophical defense and systematization of Freudian
psychoanalytic theory dealing with unconscious motivation. He attempts also to answer the charge that
the expression "unconscious motivation" is a contradiction in terms. (Psycho-Personal Approach)

707. _____. "Psychic energy and the unconscious."
Science and Methodology (1972).

708. _____. "Freud and 'unconscious motivation'."
Journal for the Theory of Social Behavior 4 (1974):
191-216. Solomon, by making a few distinctions
regarding the term "unconscious," tries to show
that the Freudian notion of unconscious motivation
is not self-contradictory. (Psycho-Personal
Approach)

709. Sorokin, Pitirim A. "Estructura mental y energías
del hombre." (Mental structure and man's ener-
gies.) Revista Mexicana de Sociologia 14, no. 1
(1952): 43-97. Sorokin presents a curious mix of
many topics. He writes about a "biological unconscious," a "sociocultural conscious," and the "supraconscious." He strongly criticizes Freud and
suggests some Hindu ideas. He also alludes to
what he called the "final personality" or the divine
within us.

710. Sperling, Melitta. "Children's interpretation and reaction to the unconscious of their mothers." International Journal of Psycho-Analysis 30 (1949): 197.
An abstract.

711. Springer, Sally P., and George Deutsch. Left Brain,
Right Brain. San Francisco: W. H. Freeman and
Company, 1981. This book provides an update on
brain research. In the speculative part of the book
the authors present the idea that some such as
D. Galin have claimed that the nondominant hemisphere is the site or foundation for the unconscious.

712. Staehelin, B. "Das marianische Unbewusste." (The
Madonna-subconscious) Praxis 71, no. 20 (May 18,
1982): 881-86. A Jungian understanding of the
unconscious is discussed.

713. Stapledon, Olaf. "A theory of the unconscious." Monist
     37 (1927): 422-43. This is a philosophical-critical
     examination of various concepts of the unconscious.
     Stapledon finds inconsistencies in all of them.
     (Psycho-Personal Approach)

714. Starr, Albert. "Psychoanalysis and the fiction of the
     unconscious." Science and Society 15 (1951): 129-
     43. Starr conducts a Marxist critique and counter-
     proposal to the Freudian theory of the unconscious.
     According to Starr the construct of the unconscious
     is a capitalist notion that cannot be accepted by
     Marxist-Leninists. In its place one can talk about
     various ways one can be unaware (ignorant) of as-
     pects of behavior or ideas. See also item no. 37.
     (Psycho-Personal Approach)

715. Starr, H. E. "Promethean constellations. Part I:
     A psychonomic contribution to analytical technique:
     Part II: Certain analytical discriminations."
     Psychological Clinic 22 (1933): 1-20. The author
     maintains that the subconscious includes the following
     contents: the drive toward self-realization, sexuali-
     ty, and the will to power. (Psycho-Personal
     Approach)

716. Steinbrechner, Edwin. Director of the D. O. M. E.
     Foundation. In Spiritual Community Guide, p. 121.
     Edited by P. S. Knalsa. San Rafael, Ca.: Spirit-
     ual Community Publications, 1978. According to
     the Guide Steinbrechner helps people find their
     Guides, that is, spiritual beings who will lead and
     protect them on journeys into the unconscious. It
     seems that Steinbrechner has woven a theory and
     practice out of ideas borrowed from Jungian psy-
     chology, Tarot practice, and astrology. It ought to
     be mentioned that many groups described in the
     Spiritual Community Guide feature "journeys" into
     the unconscious. The D. O. M. E. Foundation happens
     to be explicit about it. (Transpersonal-Spiriutal
     Approach)

717. Stern, George, and Joseph Masling. Unconscious
     Factors in Career Motivation for Teaching. Syra-
     cuse, N. Y.: Syracuse University Psychological Re-
     search Center, 1958. The authors describe three
     instruments that can be used to evaluate the uncon-
     scious factors in career motivation among teachers.
     (Psycho-Personal Approach)

718. Stettner, J. "What to do with visions." Journal of
Religion and Health 13, no. 4 (1974): 229-38. Essentially this article is a tribute to Carl Jung and
Anton Boisen. According to Stettner visions come
from the collective unconscious; are to be taken as
real; should be paid attention to, understood, and
integrated within one's life. (Transpersonal-Spiritual
Approach)

719. Steurer, William H. "A study of the relationship
between unconscious negative self concept and alcoholism: 'Positive energy release' as a comprehensive treatment approach." Ph.D. dissertation,
Union Graduate School-Midwest, 1980. This study
is based on the author's own life experience with
alcoholism, his overcoming of it, and the treatment
he developed as a result of his experience. (Psycho-
Personal Approach)

720. Steward, D. W. "Jacques Lacan and the language of
the unconscious." Bulletin of the Menninger Clinic
47, no. 1 (Jan 1983): 53-69. (Psycho-Personal
Approach)

721. Stieper, Donald R. "An experimental study of conscious
and unconscious perception." Ph.D. dissertation,
Northwestern University, 1953.

722. Stierlin, H. "Karl Jaspers' psychiatry in the light of
his basic philosophic position." Journal of the
History of the Behavioral Sciences 10, no. 2 (Apr
1974): 213-26. Stierlin presents among other
things Jaspers' criticism of Freudian theory and
practice. The criticism is based on Jaspers'
transcendentalist position and the times in which he
lived.

723. Stockmayer, W. "Figuren des kollektiven Unbewussten." (Figures of the collective unconscious.)
Zentralblatt für Psychotherapie 10 (1930): 587-98.
The author contrasts the "superpersonal unconscious" and the "personal unconscious." A Jungian
purview is assumed. The article is filled with
mythological material. (Transpersonal-Spiritual
Approach)

724. Strachey, Alix. The Unconscious Motives of War.
London: George Allen & Unwin, 1957. The book

opens with a presentation of the principles of psychoanalysis. The second part deals with Freudian
and LeBonian views regarding group psychology.
The third part offers recommendation for peace.
(Psycho-Personal and Socio-Cultural Approaches)

725. Strauss, Allan. "Unconscious mental processes and
the psychosomatic concept." International Journal
of Psychoanalysis 36 (1955): 307-19. This is
really an article about the perennial mind-body
question. Strauss presents a host of theories offered to help understand the relationship between
the mental and the physical. These theories include parallelism, interactionism, epiphenomenalism,
materialism, isomorphism, double-aspect theory,
identity theory, and field-identity theory.

726. Stross, Lawrence, and Howard Shevrin. "Hypnosis as
a method for investigating unconscious thought processes." Journal of the American Psychoanalytic
Association 17 (1969): 100-35. (Psycho-Personal
Approach)

727. Suzuki, D. T. "The unconscious in Zen Buddhism."
In Zen Buddhism and Psychoanalysis, pp. 10-23.
Edited by Erich Fromm. New York: Harper and
Brothers, 1960. According to Suzuki the "Cosmic
Unconscious" or the "Great Unconscious" is the
source of infinite creativity, and has close simili-
arities with Tao. (Transpersonal-Spiritual Approach)

728. Szondi, L. "Die Sprachen des Unbewussten: Symptom,
Symbol und Wahl." (The languages of the unconscious: symptom, symbol, and choice.) Beihefte
zur Schweizerischen Zeitschrift für Psychologie und
ihre Anwendungen no. 26 (1955): 5-34. Szondi
writes about what he called the "familial unconscious." His ideas are founded on a genetic theory
of what determines our choices. He offers a theory
to integrate and better understand the symptom
theory of Freud, the symbol theory of Jung, and
the choice theory of Szondi.

729. Tanner, Bertrand W. "The effects of conscious and
unconscious awareness on artificially induced anxiety." Ph.D. dissertation, New York University,
1953.

730. Tart, Charles T. "Subconscious." In States of Consciousness, pp. 109-14. New York: E. P. Dutton,
1975. (Psycho-Personal Approach)

731. _____. "Discrete states of consciousness." In
Symposium on Consciousness, pp. 89-175. Edited
by P. Lee, R. Ornstein, A. Deikman, and D. Galin.
New York: Viking Press, 1976. Tart presents his
model of the psyche which is patterned after the
computer model. He considers the subconscious to
be one of the subsystems comprising states of consciousness and following feedback routes. His
understanding of the subconscious is essentially
derived from both Freudian and Jungian ideas.
(Psycho-Personal Approach)

732. Tauber, Edward S., and Maurice R. Green. Prelogical
Experience: An Inquiry into Dreams and Other
Creative Processes. New York: Basic Books,
1959.

733. Tedeschi, Gianfranco. "Dall'inconscio personale di
Freud all'inconscio collettivo di Jung." (From the
personal unconscious of Freud to the collective unconscious of Jung.) Rassegna Neuropsichiat 4, no.
2 (1950): 103-11. The author compares the two
constructs in question. (Psycho-Personal and
Transpersonal-Spiritual Approaches)

734. Thomae, H. "Experimentelle Beiträge zum Problem
der unbewussten Sinneseindrücke." (Experimental
contributions to the problem of unconscious sensory
impressions.) Zeitschrift für angewandte Psychologie 60 (1941): 346-83. The study produced some
evidence in favor of unconscious sensory perception.
(Bio-Physical Approach)

735. Thomas, W. I. "The configurations of personality."
In The Unconscious, A Symposium pp. 143-77.
Edited by C. M. Child. New York: Alfred A.
Knopf, 1927. Thomas contends that personality is
in part determined by both the conservative and
creative function of the unconscious.

736. Thornburn, J. M. Art and the Unconscious, A Psychological Approach to a Problem of Philosophy.
London: Kegan Paul, 1925.

737. Thouless, R. "Soul beliefs and hypotheses." Mind 33
(1924): 262-74. Thouless mentions that the term
"unconscious" is like the word "soul" in that both
are interpreted in various ways and used to cover
a wide variety of events. Although his topic is
primarily the soul, his program for clarifying the
term applies equally well toward efforts to avoid
confusion regarding the construct of the unconscious.

738. Thur, Robert. "Longing for union: The Doppelganger
in Wuthering Heights and Frankenstein." Ph.D.
dissertation, California School of Professional
Psychology, San Francisco, 1976. This is an
archetypal-phenomenological analysis of the Doppelganger, which is seen as symbol of the deep and
unconscious internal divisions of the psyche as well
as the quest for the Self.

739. Tikhomirov, O. K. ["Theoretical problems of research
on the unconscious."] Voprosy Psikhologii no. 2
(Mar-Apr 1981): 31-39. The author argues in
favor of a dialectic materialist understanding of the
unconscious, and an understanding in terms of set
theory. (Bio-Physical and Psycho-Personal
Approaches)

740. Tomkin, Silvan S. "Consciousness and the unconscious
in a model of the human being." Acta Psychologica
11 (1955): 160-61.

741. Toole, Elizabeth W. "Maternal conflict and the emo-
tionally disturbed child: The effects of unconscious
maternal conflict on the abilities of clinic children
to resolve conflict in structured doll-play situations."
Ph.D. dissertation, California School of Professional
Psychology, Los Angeles, 1976. Results indicate
that children who were related to their mother's
unconscious conflicts do demonstrate greater dis-
turbance in their task performance. (Psycho-
Personal Approach)

742. Tourov, Nisan. B'yod'im uv'lo yod'im. (Conscious
and unconscious.) Jerusalem: Bialik Institute of
the Jewish Agency for Palestine, 1946. Tourov
distinguishes a "spiritual world" and a "real world."
He discusses the role of unconsciousness in creative
thinking, art, misunderstanding, senility, war and

peace, and the happiness of people. He also presents ideas concerning the unconscious background
of various psychological types.

743. Trotter, Wilfred. Instinct of the Herd in Peace and
War. London: Oxford University Press, 1953.
The author has a socio-cultural understanding of the
unconscious.

744. Turner, Charles C. "Primordial format: Archetypal
symbols of the unconscious in a science fiction
television series." Ph.D. dissertation, New York
University, 1973. Turner draws on the ideas of
Jung and Neumann in order to analyze the symbolic
content and patterns in the television series "Voyage
to the Bottom of the Sea" (1964-68). (Socio-Cultural
Approach)

745. Tusquets, J. "La vida no conscient." (The unconscious mental life.) Criterion 10 (1934): 247-50.
The author lists unconscious mechanisms and their
influence on mental life. (Psycho-Personal Approach)

746. Ulanov, Ann. "God and Depth Psychology." In God in
Contemporary Thought, pp. 939-56. Edited by
S. A. Matczak. New York: Learned Publications,
Inc., 1977. Ulanov discusses how a psychology of
the unconscious can help to humanize religion, and
how through the unconscious one can rediscover
religious truths. (Transpersonal-Spiritual Approach)

747. _____, and Barry Ulanov. Religion and the Unconscious. Philadelphia: Westminster Press, 1975.
This book represents an interface between psychology and religion according to two Jungians.

748. Umriukhin, E. A. "Sistemnye mekhanizmy podsozatel'-
noi deiatel nosti cheloveka." (Systems mechanisms
of human subconscious activity.) Vestnik Akademii
Meditsinskikh Nauk 2 (1982): 88-95. The author
employs a bio-physical approach regarding the unconscious.

749. Valentine, C. W. The New Psychology of the Unconscious. London: Christophers, 1928. This is a
republication of the author's previous work Dreams
and the Unconscious. Valentine is working with

the principles of psychoanalysis. (Psycho-Personal
Approach)

750. Vallone, Gerard F. "The unconscious dimensions of
Dewey's moral philosophy." Ph.D. dissertation,
Fordham University, 1979. According to Vallone,
Dewey recognized the existence of unconscious aspects of experiencing but never systematized his
ideas on the topic. Vallone also relates the work
of Dewey to that of Freud and draws some conclu-
sions for the process of education. (Psycho-
Personal Approach)

751. Van den Daele, L. "Discussion of 'Structuralism in
Psychoanalysis'." American Journal of Psychoanalysis 39, no. 4 (1979): 353-57. The author is
responding to the paper by M. Rendon. (See M.
Rendon.) The topic is the role of the unconscious
in the structuralist approach. (Psycho-Personal
Approach)

752. Van der Hoop, Johannes H. Character and the Unconscious. College Park, Md.: McGrath Publishing, 1970. The author draws on the ideas of
Freud and Jung.

753. Van der Horst, L. "Lessen in de hedendaagsche psychologie. IV. Over den aard van het onbewusste."
(Lessons in contemporary psychology. IV. The
nature of the unconscious.) Nederlandsch tijdschrift
voor psychologie 3 (1935): 129-35. The author
compares some ideas of Freud with those of
Nietzsche, such as "superman" and "herd-idea."

754. Van Dusen, W. The Natural Depth in Man. New York:
Harper & Row, 1972. A Swedenborgian point of
view. (Transpersonal-Spiritual Approach)

755. Van Rappard, J. F. "Romantic psychology."
Tijdschrift voor Psychologie 6, no. 3-4 (1978):
157-80. This is a good history on the Enlighten-
ment and Romantic movements vis-à-vis the idea of
the unconscious. The author maintains that the Romantic understanding of the unconscious supplemented
the idea of the isolated ego of the enlightened individual.

756. Vargiu, J. "Creativity." Synthesis (1977): 17-53.
     The author discusses the relationship between the
     unconscious and the creative process.

757. [Various]. "Leitsätze de Vorträge und Referate des IV
     Allgemeinen ärztlichen Kongresses für Psychothera-
     pie in Bad Nauheim vom 12-14 April, 1929." (Ab-
     stracts and reports of the Fourth General Congress
     for Psychotherapy in Bad Nauheim April 12-14,
     1929.) Allgemeine ärztliche Zeitschrift für Psycho-
     therapie und psychische Hygiene 2 (1929): 129-56.
     Some of the relevant papers include the following:
     1) Korner, "The clinical significance of the collect-
     ive unconscious"; 2) W. Schindler, "Dream inter-
     pretation in the light of the different psychological
     schools of the unconscious, and their clinical sig-
     nificance." Carl Jung also presented a paper at
     this meeting: "Goals of Psychotherapy."

758. Velikovsky, I. "Kann eine neuerlernte Sprache zur
     Sprache des Unbewussten werden?" (Can a second
     language become the language of the unconscious?)
     Imago, Lpz. 20 (1934): 234-39. Hebrew is the
     language in question. (Psycho-Personal Approach)

759. _____. "Jeu de mots hébraiques. Une langue nou-
     vellement acquise peut-elle devenir la langue de
     l'inconscient?" (Hebraic play on words. Can a
     newly acquired language become the language of the
     unconscious?) Revue française de psychanalyse 10,
     no. 1 (1938). (Psycho-Personal Approach)

760. Victoroff, D. "Le concept du 'role' et la notion d'in-
     conscient." (The concept of the 'role' and the idea
     of the unconscious.) Psyché 6 (1951): 630-39.
     The author speaks of an unconscious that stores a
     multitude of social roles. This work is based on
     the ideas of Cooley, Mead, and Couter. (Psycho-
     Personal Approach)

761. Viterbi, Mirjam. "Unconscious Jewish contents in
     Catholic patients of Jewish ancestry." Mental Health
     and Society 2, no. 3-6 (1975): 175-80. With three
     case studies Viterbi makes the point that a Jewish
     unconscious, once formed, persists and continues to
     influence behavior despite an individual's later change

of religion.　(Psycho-Personal and Socio-Cultural
Approaches)

762.　Von Franz, Marie Louise.　Projection and Recollection
in Jungian Psychology.　LaSalle, Ill.:　Open Court,
1980.

763.　Von Stern, M. R.　Theorie des Unbewussten.　(Theory
of the Unconscious.)　Linz a/D:　F. Steurer, 1929.
The author presents a theory of the unconscious
which contends it is the original creative power
pervading all things and all people.　There's no
doubt of the transpersonal-spiritual approach assumed here.

764.　Voronin, L. G., and V. F. Konovalov.　"Fiziologiches-
ki analiz vzaimodeistviya osoznannykh i neosoznan-
nykh sledovykh protsessov pri otschete vremeni."
(Physiological analysis of the interaction of conscious and unconscious trace processes in estimating
time.)　Zhurnal Vysshei Nervnoi Deyatel'nosti 20,
no. 5 (Sept 1970):　899-907.　(Bio-Physical
Approach)

765.　Wahba, M.　["Bergson's view on the unconscious."]
(In Arabic).　Egyptian Journal of Psychology 8
(1952-53):　213-22.　According to Wahba, Bergson
understood the unconscious to be the relation between spirit and body as manifested in memory.
It is not the result of primary instinctual drive but
of what a person puts into his or her mind.
(Psycho-Personal Approach)

766.　Waites, E. A.　"Female self representation and the
unconscious:　A reply to Amy Galen."　Psychoanalytic Review 69, no. 1 (Spring 1982):　29-41.　Amy
Galen, an orthodox psychoanalyst, contended that
the unconscious meaning of being female is defined
primarily by anatomy and hence relatively unchange-
able despite social changes.　Waites, an ego psychologist, argues that it is not so and that being
female has more to do with ego-function and not
id-functions.　(Bio-Physical and Psycho-Personal
Approaches)

767.　Wake, Margaret B.　"Unconscious response to sexual
symbols."　Ph.D. dissertation, Wayne State Univer-

sity, 1966. This is an experimental study designed
to demonstrate the operation of unconscious thought
processes, and to support psychoanalytic postulates
regarding unconscious responses in transference and
dreaming. (Psycho-Personal Approach)

768. Waldstein, Louis. The Subconscious Self. New York:
Scribner's Sons, 1926. According to Waldstein
each of us has a conscious self and an unconscious
self. The former is related to the outer world,
the latter to the inner world. The subconscious
self is the product and accumulation of all impressions deposited in our memory from birth, and
which continue to influence our life in subtle ways.
(Psycho-Personal and Transpersonal-Spiritual
Approaches)

769. Walker, A. "Music and the unconscious." British
Medical Journal 2, no. 6205 (Dec 22-29, 1979):
1641-43. This article is based on a psychoanalytic
theory of the unconscious. (Psycho-Personal
Approach)

770. Walker, Nigel. "Science and the Freudian unconscious."
Psychoanalysis 4, no. 4 (1957): 117-24. In this
pro-Freudian article Wallace contends that the
Freudian unconscious is a respectable, scientific
and explanatory model that is useful to the psycho-
therapist in order to make sense of certain behavior.
(Psycho-Personal Approach)

771. Wallace, W. "Some dimensions of creativity." Personnel Journal 46, no. 7, part I & II (1967): 363-
70, 438-43, 458. In discussing creativity Wallace
draws on the ideas of Maslow to say that the unconscious is not merely a negative aspect of a
person, but it is also the source of creativeness,
and even of certain kinds of truth and knowledge.

772. Wallon, Henri. La conscience et la vie subconsciente.
(Consciousness and the subconscious.) Paris:
Presses Universitaires de France, 1942.

773. Watson, Edmund H. Unconscious Humorist and Other
Essays. Freeport, N.Y.: Books for Libraries
Press, 1973. Originally printed in 1896.

774. Watson, John B. "The unconscious of the behaviorist."
     In The Unconscious, A Symposium, pp. 91-113.
     Edited by C. M. Child. New York: Alfred A.
     Knopf, 1927. Watson rejects the concept of the un-
     conscious. He would prefer to consider that the
     concept refers to the system of nonverbalized habits
     that are developed in infancy. He is particularly
     harsh on Freud. (Bio-Physical Approach)

775. _____. "The myth of the unconscious." Harper's
     Magazine 155 (1927): 502-8. This is another ren-
     dition of Watson's rejection of the construct of the
     unconscious. (Bio-Physical Approach)

776. Watson, J. P. "An experimental method for the study
     of unconscious conflict." British Journal of Medical
     Psychology 48 (1975): 299-301. The paper is a
     response to the work of Lloyd Silverman. The
     method involves tachistoscopic stimulation and the
     measurement of the effect. The results are held
     to support various hypotheses concerning psycho-
     pathology derived from psychoanalytic theory.
     (Bio-Physical and Psycho-Personal Approaches)

777. Watt, A. W. "Investigation and treatment of early
     mental disorders." Medical Press 207 (1942): 270-
     74. Watt presents case studies involving anxiety,
     obsession, and dreams related to unconscious striv-
     ings. In one place he refers to a man who had a
     western education superimposed on his "eastern
     unconscious." (Psycho-Personal and Socio-Cultural
     Approaches)

778. Watts, Alan. "Asian psychology and modern psychia-
     try." American Journal of Psychoanalysis 13, no.
     25 (1953). Watts discusses the affinity of the notion
     of Tao with the concept of the unconscious. He
     makes the point that the orientals tend to trust the
     unconscious whereas in the West we tend to want
     to control it. (Psycho-Personal and Transpersonal-
     Spiritual Approaches)

779. Weinberg, Henry. "An investigation of unconscious
     conflict in cases of peptic ulcer." Ph. D. disserta-
     tion, Harvard University, 1951. (Psycho-Personal
     Approach)

780. Weiner, Melvin. The Cognitive Unconscious: A Piaget-
     ian Approach to Psychotherapy. Davis, Cal.: In-
     ternational Psychological Press, 1975. This ap-
     proach involves the use of cognitive tasks as a way
     to surface and work with affective mechanisms.
     (Psycho-Personal Approach)

781. Weisskopf, W. A. "Existential crisis and the uncon-
     scious." Journal of Humanistic Psychology 7, no.
     1 (1967): 58-65. (Psycho-Personal Approach)

782. Welwood, John H. "A theoretical re-interpretation of
     the concept of the unconscious from a humanistic
     and phenomenological perspective." Ph.D. disser-
     tation, University of Chicago, 1974. Welwood of-
     fers to replace the construct of the unconscious
     with the idea of organismic structurings of the
     world which function as a ground of focal attention.
     He derives a whole new list of terms and definitions
     and proceeds to use that vocabulary to reinterpret
     various phenomena, such as meditation, creativity,
     and mysticism. Much of his work is based on the
     principles of Gestalt psychology. (Psycho-Personal
     Approach)

783. _____. "Exploring mind: Form, emptiness, and
     beyond." Journal of Transpersonal Psychology 8,
     no. 2 (1976): 89-99. Welwood proposes a three-
     level model of the mind which includes "differen-
     tiated mind," "undifferentiated mind," and "back-
     ground environment." (Psycho-Personal and
     Transpersonal-Spiritual Approaches)

784. Wenzl, A. Das unbewusste Denken. (Unconscious
     thought.) Karlsruhe: G. Braun, 1927. Wenzl
     investigates the question of whose thought is it
     when an intuition erupts. He argues that the as-
     sumption of an impersonal unconscious is less
     suitable than the assumption of a soul. Ultimately
     Wenzl discusses the entelechy hypothesis of Driesch.
     (Transpersonal-Spiritual Approach)

785. Wenzl, Aloys. "Erinnerungsarbeit bei erschwerter
     Wortfindung und das Probelm des Unterbewussten."
     (Difficulties in word-recall and the problem of the
     unconscious.) Jahrbuch für Psychologie und Psy-

chotherapie 1 (1952): 108-16. Wenzl explores the
intervening responses and processes that can facilitate the recall of a word. (Psycho-Personal
Approach)

786. Weszely, O. "A tudatalatti lelki étlet és a nevelés."
(Subconscious mental life and education.) Gyermek
27 (1935): 1-3, 14-33. The author presents and
critiques the ideas of Freud, Adler, and Jung. Regarding education Weszely maintains that the child
ought to be taught to inhibit certain behaviors and
be raised up for the betterment of humanity.
(Psycho-Personal Approach)

787. Whitaker, Carl, and Augustus Napier. The Family
Crucible. New York: Harper & Row, 1978. This
is a study in systems theory in the service of family therapy. The authors refer to the unconscious
influences and dimensions of a particular family as
"The Family." This "Family" acts as if it were
an invisible member of the family in question, and
exerts its influence. (Socio-Cultural Approach)

788. White, Ernest. Christian Life and the Unconscious.
New York: Harper & Brothers, 1955. The book
is essentially about the workings of the Holy Spirit
in the life of a Christian. When White uses the
expression "unconscious" he is really referring to
the hidden life of the Spirit. There is very little
theoretical discussion of the unconscious and the
author uses the term rather loosely; that is, he
uses it as a noun, an adverb, and as an adjective.
He suggests that the unconscious is the medium for
prayers, our connection to God, and the starting
point and setting for salvation within the person's
heart. (Transpersonal-Spiritual Approach)

789. White, Victor. God and the Unconscious. London:
Harvill Press, 1952. This book represents a dream
come true for Carl Jung; that is, that a theologian
would take his theory of the unconscious seriously.
White takes Jung's ideas seriously and attempts to
conduct a psychological-theological synthesis. One
of the chapters deals with the question of revelation.
(Transpersonal-Spiritual Approach)

790. _____. Soul and Psyche. London: Collins and
Harvill Press, 1960. This is another attempt by

White to interface a psychology of the unconscious
(à la Jung) with religious topics. (Transpersonal-
Spiritual Approach)

791. White, William A. "Primitive mentality and the racial
unconscious." American Journal of Psychiatry 4
(1924-25): 663-71. White uses the expressions
"fore-conscious," "personal unconscious," and "racial unconscious." It is the last category that in-
terests White. He points out that the racial unconscious is a real factor to consider when treating
mental illnesses. The psyche is as old as the body
and has its own history of development. (Socio-
Cultural Approach)

792. _____. "Higher levels of mental integration." In
The Unconscious, A Symposium, pp. 242-60. Edited by C. M. Child. New York: Alfred A. Knopf,
1927. White understands the unconscious as an
influencer of development in terms of the subtle conflicts and adjustments between race-preservative and
self-preservative tendencies within the person.
(Psycho-Personal and Socio-Cultural Approaches)

793. Whitmont, E. C. "The approach to the unconscious."
In The Symbolic Quest. Princeton, N.J.: Princeton University Press, 1969. This is a Jungian
approach to the topic.

794. Whyte, Lancelot L. The Unconscious Before Freud.
New York: Basic Books, Inc., 1960. This is a
landmark historical work on the idea of the unconscious before Freud. (Psycho-Personal and
Transpersonal-Spiritual Approaches)

795. _____. Encyclopedia of Philosophy. S. v. "Unconscious." This is a highly abbreviated version of
the book previously cited.

796. Wickes, F. C. The Inner World of Man. New York:
Frederick Ungar Publishing, 1948. In this work
Wickes writes about the unconscious as a substratum
that contains all the contents of the psyche of which
we are unaware at any given moment. He also refers to a "Mother Lode" out of which consciousness
is mined. A Jungian framework is assumed.
(Psycho-Personal and Transpersonal-Spiritual
Approaches)

797. Wikse, John R. "About possession: Essays on the politics of the possessive unconscious." Ph. D. dissertation, University of California, Berkeley, 1973.

798. Wilbur, George B. "A psychoanalyst's ruminations on an epistemological problem." In Psychoanalysis and Culture, pp. 295-318. Edited by G. B. Wilbur and W. Muensterberger. New York: International Universities Press, 1951. This is a discussion of the logic of our conscious and the "logic" of our unconscious. The former is the stuff of psychology, the latter the stuff of metapsychology. (Psycho-Personal Approach)

799. Wilbur, Kenneth. "Psychologia perennis: The spectrum of consciousness." Journal of Transpersonal Psychology 7, no. 2 (1975): 105-32. (Psycho-Personal and Transpersonal-Spiritual Approaches)

800. _____. The Spectrum of Consciousness. Wheaton, Ill. Quest, 1977.

801. _____. "A developmental view of consciousness." Journal of Transpersonal Psychology 11, no. 1 (1979): 1-21. Wilbur presents his "map" of the psyche which includes the following: 1) Ground-Unconscious, which has to do with the deep structures of the mind; 2) Archaic-Unconscious, which is related to what Freud and Jung have written on the topic; 3) Submergent-Unconscious, which is the suppressed, repressed unconscious; 4) Embedded-Unconscious, which is akin to the superego and all that we unconsciously identify with and perceive the world with; and 5) Emergent-Unconscious, which has the potential for transpersonal-spiritual experiences. (Psycho-Personal and Transpersonal-Spiritual Approaches)

802. Williams, J. K. The Wisdom of Your Subconscious Mind. Englewood Cliffs, N.J.: Prentice-Hall Inc., 1964. (Transpersonal-Spiritual Approach)

803. _____. The Knack of Using Your Subconscious Mind. Englewood Cliffs, N.J.: Prentice-Hall, Inc. 1958. (Transpersonal-Spiritual Approach)

804. Wilmer, Harry A. "'You know': Observations on in-
      terjectory, seemingly meaningless phrases in group
      psychotherapy." Psychiatric Quarterly 41, no. 2
      (1967): 296-323. Seemingly meaningless phrases
      often reveal/hide unconscious material. In a sense
      Wilmer is suggesting that such phrases can be
      treated as "roads" to the unconscious. (Psycho-
      Personal Approach)

805. Wilson, R. A. "Mere coincidence." Science Digest
      (Jan 1982): 83-95. Wilson refers to Jung's theory
      of the collective unconscious in discussing the ques-
      tion of coincidences. (Transpersonal-Spiritual
      Approach)

806. Wisdom, J. "The unconscious origin of Schopenhauer's
      philosophy." International Journal of Psycho-
      Analysis 26 (1945): 44-52. Wisdom attempts an
      unmasking of Schopenhauer's philosophy by arguing
      that it was a manifestation of unconscious forces
      within the philosopher as well as the defenses
      against those forces. (Psycho-Personal Approach)

807. Wiseman, Richard J. "The Rorschach as a stimulus
      for hypnotic dreams: A study of unconscious pro-
      cesses." Ph.D. dissertation, Michigan State Uni-
      versity, 1962. This study is based on Freudian
      dream theory and is consistent with Freud's theory
      of the "dreamwork." Wiseman wants to show that
      the Rorschach test is a useful technique for the
      laboratory of dreams. (Psycho-Personal Approach)

808. Wolf, Robert. "The Polaroid technique: Spontaneous
      dialogues from the unconscious." Art Psychotherapy
      3 (1976): 197-214. Wolf offers another "road" to
      the unconscious this time using a Polaroid camera.
      The process really involves free association but
      facilitated by photographs taken of the patient and/or
      therapist. The idea is that photographs can help
      where words fail to start the process of free asso-
      ciation. (Psycho-Personal Approach)

809. Wolff, D. "Diskussionsbemerkungen zu dem aufsatz
      von D. Müller-Hegemann 'Bermerkungen zur narko-
      analyse'." (Discussion of the article "Remarks on
      Narcoanalysis" by D. Müller-Hegemann.) Müller-

Hegemann, D. "Antwort auf die Diskussionsbemerkung von D. Wolff." (Answer to the discussion by D. Wolff.) Psychiatrie Neurologie und medizinische Psychologie 6 (1954): 247-49. Wolff critiques the Müller-Hegemann's argument against the assumption of the unconscious and of archetypes. Müller-Hegemann stresses the role of consciousness and is very critical of depth psychology. The discussion is based on the use of drugs in psychotherapy. (Psycho-Personal Approach)

810. Wolff, Werner. "Ein Forschungsbericht. Grundlegung einer experimentaellen Tiefenpsychologie." (A research report. Foundation of an experimental psychology of the unconscious.) Imago 20, no. 1 (1934). Wolff suggests that one could conduct a more accurate analysis of someone if one studied the person without that person's knowledge. Also it would be better if a number of judges worked on the same person thereby reducing the subjectivity factor of only one interpretation. (Bio-Physical and Psycho-Personal Approaches)

811. _____. Diagrams of the Unconscious, Handwriting and Personality in Measurement, Experiment and Analysis. There is very little theoretical or otherwise discussion of the unconscious per se. The word is hardly used. The book is really about the foundations for handwriting analysis and should have been entitled so. The point made is that handwriting can be used in diagnosing personality. Wolff is suggesting another "road" to the unconscious. (Bio-Physical and Psycho-Personal Approaches)

812. Wolman, B. B. The Unconscious Mind. Englewood Cliffs, N. J.: Prentice-Hall, Inc., 1968. The author is working within a Freudian framework. (Psycho-Personal Approach)

813. Wolstein, Benjamin. "The psychoanalytic theory of unconscious psychic experience." Contemporary Psychoanalysis 18, no. 3 (Jul 1982): 412-37. The author contends that the psychoanalytic theory needs to be updated. (Psycho-Personal Approach)

814. Woodman, R. W. "Creativity as a construct in personality theory." Journal of Creative Behavior

(Spr 1981): 43-67. In discussing creativity Woodman explains how an understanding of the unconscious within a particular theory relates to the creative process. He mentions Freud, Jung, and
others. (Psycho-Personal and Transpersonal-
Spiritual Approaches)

815. Woodworth, H. "Report of investigations into an obscure function of the subconscious mind." Journal
of American Social Psychology Research 36 (1942):
185-230. Experimental evidence regarding ESP
is presented. Woodworth maintains that the subconscious mind may be responsible for the phenomena of ESP. (Psycho-Personal and Transpersonal-
Spiritual Approaches)

816. Wyschogrod, Michael. "Sartre, freedom and the unconscious." Review of Existential Psychology and
Psychiatry 1 (1961): 179-86. The author discusses
the threat to the ideal and idea of human freedom
that the Freudian understanding of the unconscious
represents. Wyschogrod takes up Sartre's argument
of self-deception against the theory of the unconscious. Wyschogrod concludes that the individual
is free and responsible. The task of psychotherapy
is to bring to conscious light that which is not yet
realized by consciousness. (Psycho-Personal
Approach)

817. Zeigler, Harley H. "Some aspects of the concept of
unconscious purpose in modern philosophy." Ph.D.
dissertation, Boston University Graduate School,
1940.

818. Zilboorg, G. "The fundamental conflict with psychoanalysis." International Journal of Psycho-Analysis
20 (1939): 480-92. Zilboorg contends that the fundamental source of opposition to psychoanalysis
stems from the confusion between the psychological
construct "psyche" and the theological concept of
"Soul," and the anxiety that such a confusion
arouses. (Psycho-Personal Approach)

819. _____. A History of Medical Psychology. New
York: W. W. Norton, 1941. In various places
there is mention of the idea of the unconscious.
(Psycho-Personal Approach)

820. Zulliger, H. Unbewusstes Seelenleben. (Unconscious mental life.) Stuttgart: Franckh'sche Verlagshandlung, 1926. This short book provides the basics of psychoanalysis to be used by physicians and teachers in interpreting the behavior of their patients or students. (Psycho-Personal Approach)

821. Zweig, A. "Über die psychischen Leistungen eines Hundes und deren mögliche Beziehungen zur Human-Psychologie." (On the psychic performances of the dog and their possible relationship to human psychology.) Schweizerische Zeitschrift für Psychologie und ihre Anwendungen 16 (1957): 1-16. This is a curious discussion of a dog's unconscious, and how dog psychology can inform human psychology. Essentially Zweig is working within the Freudian system of ideas regarding the unconscious. (Bio-Physical and Psycho-Personal Approaches)

---

*Although not mentioned within this bibliography, one could also re-
late the construct of the unconscious with the notion of Panentheism.

Projection 268, 556, 762
Promethean constellations 715
Proper consciousness 119
Psi 618
Psyche 372
Psychic energy 707
Psychoanalysis 11, 21, 43,
    72, 103, 106, 114, 137,
    138, 145, 162, 168, 178,
    193, 197, 204, 214, 221,
    238, 240, 247, 250, 252,
    264, 283, 331, 365, 409,
    432, 434, 439, 440, 447,
    450, 461, 473, 474, 489,
    501, 521, 586, 604, 616,
    633, 662, 727, 751, 798,
    818, 820
Psychologism 687
"Psychonauts" 519
Psychopathology 364
Psychosis 173, 517
Psychosomatics 134
Psychosynthesis 26, 27, 301,
    302, 516
Psychotic speech 504

Racism 529; See also Preju-
    dice
Radilova, J. 601
Rank, Otto 111, 438
Rational 196, 270, 279, 315,
    322
Realms of the unconscious
    170, 290, 466
Reflexes 607, 613
Religious studies 61, 62, 101,
    106, 135, 151, 167, 192,
    202, 218, 219, 242, 250,
    252, 272, 274, 275, 294,
    301, 312, 332, 345, 347,
    350, 356, 377, 378, 380,
    381, 402, 403, 404, 407,
    409, 438, 454, 459, 465,
    473, 474, 492, 531, 532,
    533, 566, 569, 570, 575,
    582, 649, 718, 746, 747,
    761, 788, 789, 790
Rendon, M. 751
Repression 122, 264, 266,
    301, 334, 361, 422, 560,
    606, 631, 660
Resistance 469

Resnicke, Robert 622
Responsibility 54, 527, 551,
    599; See also Autonomy
Revelation 219, 402, 789
Ribot, Theodore 353, 412
Ricoeur, Paul 195, 473
Rilke, Rainer Maria 411
Ring, Kenneth 466
Ritualism 449
Rivers, W. H. R. 150
Rogers, Carl 147, 541
Rolfing 608
Romanticism 48, 105, 304,
    315, 755
Rorschach test 205, 491, 807
Royal Road (to the unconscious)
    113, 141, 205, 284, 288,
    290, 456, 491, 501, 564,
    622, 626, 675, 684, 702,
    804, 808, 811
Ryle 285, 691

Sadism 287
Sadock, B. 283, 393
Salanter, Israel 272
Salvation 562, 570, 788
Sanchez, Jaen 565
Sapir, E. 520
Sartre, Jean-Paul 129, 175,
    361, 393, 422, 816
Schafer 20
Schelling, Friedrich 313
Schindler, W. 757
Schizophrenia 186, 396, 503
Schmidt, Arno 163
Schopenhauer, Arthur 330,
    806
Schur, Max 426
Science 255, 770
Science fiction 744
Scientology 340
Sechenov, I. 10
Secondary non-conscious 348
Seele 53
Self 26, 51, 73, 90, 141,
    175, 186, 200, 281, 286,
    315, 342, 361, 391, 393,
    395, 407, 420, 436, 441,
    488, 506, 508, 516, 538,
    560, 567, 568, 605, 606,
    621, 643, 671, 715, 719,
    738, 766, 768, 792, 816

Unconscious (adjective) [cont.]
  insight 79, 313, 512
  intention 695, 697
  Jewish contents 761
  knowledge 404
  life 619
  material 540, 804
  mental life 820, 745
  mental representation 666
  mental states 130, 349
  mentation 189
  mind see Mind
  moral judgment 467
  motivation see Motivation
  mystical communication
    688
  patterning 659
  perception 254, 581; See
    also Perception
  personality 363
  phenomena 353, 399, 425
  preference 155
  prejudice 29
  processes 76, 148, 169,
    214, 256, 322, 479, 510,
    513, 514, 521, 601, 615,
    725, 807
  psychic experience 813
  purpose 817
  rebel 400
  remembrance 623
  resistance 133, 442
  response 767
  self-judgment 342
  sense of time 518
  sensory impression 734
  sexual identity 542
  sexual stereotyping 423
  states 349, 350, 607
  stimuli 144
  structure 139, 159, 520,
    700
  suicide 164, 499
  tendencies 456
  thought 576, 726, 767,
    784
  trace processes 764
  verse mechanism 674
  whispering 405
  wishes 268, 655, 656
Unconscious (word used as a
    noun)
  Absolute 105, 304

Acquired 650
Aesthetic 290, 523, 524
Affective 574
Archaic 801
Automatic 523, 524
Awakened 647
Biological 182, 281, 709
Cognitive 574, 780
Collective see Collective
  Unconscious
Common 463
Configurational 50
Conservative 326
Cosmic 686, 727
Creative 35, 546, 651
Deep Psychological 182
Distant 650
Dog's 821
Dynamic 182, 523, 524
Dynamic Psychological 318
Eastern 777
Embedded 801
Emergent 801
Emotional 196
Extraterrestrial 623
Familial 543, 728
Forgetful 512
Freudian 195, 235, 239,
  265, 401, 434, 457, 548,
  568, 577, 620, 650, 686,
  770
Great 727
Ground 801
Higher 26, 301, 466, 516
Impersonal 784
Inattentive 512
Incommunicable 512
Inherited 512
Innate 650
Insightless 512
Instinctive 669
Instinctual 218
Involuntary 512
Jewish 761
Living 447
Lower 26, 516
Metaphysical 182
Middle 26, 516
More accessible psycholo-
  gical 182
Musical 154
Observable 613
Ontogenetic 623

Unconscious (noun) [cont.]
  Palingenetic 650
  Partial Absolute 105
  Perinatal 290
  Personal 302, 632, 723,
    733, 790
  Phylogenetic 623
  Physical 318
  Physiological 50, 304, 318
  Possessive 797
  Psychic 89, 281
  Psychoanalytic 4, 391
  Psychodynamic 290, 623
  Psychological 89, 304,
    435, 692, 693
  Racial 321, 678, 791
  Rational 196
  Relative 105
  Repressed 293, 558, 606,
    644, 677, 801
  Spiritual 218
  Subliminal 512
  Submergent 801
  Superpersonal 723
  Transcendent 218
  Trans-Individual 623
  Transpersonal 290
  True 444
  Universal 557
  Vital 294
Unconsciousism 650
Unconsciousness 631
Universal Forms 126
Unknown Self 286
Utopia 423
Uznadze, D. N. 99, 121,
  429, 510

Vienna decadence 187, 188
Velikovsky, M. 576
Visions 475, 488, 718
Vitalistic Biology 447
Vocational choice 70, 343
Void 623
Vortex theory 316

Waelder 507
Walpole, Horace 300
Walter, E. Dale 141
War 45, 214, 724, 742, 743
Welty, Eudora 24
White, Victor 378
Wholeness 341
Wilbur, G. B. 798
Wilhelm, R. 388
Will to power 715
Wittgenstein, Ludwig 461,
  567
Wolff-Huntley technique 395
Wolfgang, Rock 14
Wood, Mrs. Henry 305
Word presentation 58
World peace 701

Yoga 204, 608

Zen 252, 391, 727
Ziehen 435